The Efficacy of Law

The Efficacy
of Law

Harry W. Jones

1968 ROSENTHAL LECTURES
Northwestern University School of Law

NORTHWESTERN UNIVERSITY PRESS
Evanston, Illinois

Copyright © 1969 by Northwestern University Press
Library of Congress Catalog Card Number: 79-89822
SBN: 8101-0263-3
All rights reserved
Manufactured in the United States of America

Harry W. Jones is Cardozo Professor of Jurisprudence at the Columbia University School of Law.

Preface

THIS BRIEF NOTE, mislabeled as a preface, is really an expression of my gratitude to the faculty and the students of the Northwestern University School of Law. It is an uncommon privilege to deliver the Rosenthal Lectures, particularly when one follows soon after such lecturers as Justice Walter V. Schaefer and Judge Carl McGowan. I am particularly mindful of the tradition of excellence maintained throughout the twenty years of the Rosenthal lectureship, because my own research and teaching interests give me frequent occasion to consult books that had their origin as Rosenthal Lectures. Paul Freund's *On Understanding the Supreme Court* (1949), Willard Hurst's *Law and the Conditions of Freedom in the Nineteenth Century United States* (1956), and Harold Havighurst's *The Nature of Private Contract* (1961) are three of the best-thumbed volumes on my bookshelf.

So I was deeply appreciative of the invitation extended to me by my friends of the law faculty to give the 1968 Rosenthal Lectures.

I am equally grateful to Northwestern's law students for the generous hearing they gave me when these lectures were delivered on December 2, 3, and 4, 1968, and for their lively and perceptive comments and criticisms at informal meetings after each lecture. Some controversial points are touched on in these lectures, particularly in my third, and my student friends, when their time to be heard came, expressed their occasional disagreements candidly and forcefully, but always with complete fairness and courtesy. Nobody lost his temper, nobody engaged in personalities, nobody raised his voice. I came away from these sessions with many more ideas than I had brought to Chicago with me. I came away, too, with the conviction that the intellectual and moral education of men and women for the public profession of the law is going wonderfully well at Northwestern.

HARRY W. JONES

Contents

I. MAKING LAWS AND INFLUENCING PEOPLE:
The Province of Jurisprudence
and the World Outside *1*

II. PRECEPTS AND CONSEQUENCES:
The Uneven Correspondence
of Lawmaking Purpose and Social Outcome *37*

III. CONSTITUTIONALISM AND DISOBEDIENCE:
The Law and Politics of Domestic Tranquility *67*

I

Making Laws and Influencing People:

The Province of Jurisprudence and the World Outside

LAW IS BEHAVIORAL. The construction of legal precepts—call them rules, commands, norms, or what you will—is not a form of art for art's sake but an enterprise designed to influence the behavior of people. Many of these precepts are addressed, exclusively or largely, to such people as judges and other public officials and are, in effect, directions or authorizations as to how they should or may proceed in the discharge of their public responsibilities. Other legal precepts have a farther reach and set, or undertake to set, patterns of behavior for citizens generally, standards of conduct to be observed by individual members of society in their relations with each other and with the agencies of the state. A constitutional, statutory, or case-law precept has *efficacy* in a society to the extent that the actual behavior of the people who compose the society, both officials and the generality of private citizens, conforms to the standards which the precept directs or authorizes. A legal precept that is not observed is like a piece of music never played, an offer that has languished for want of an acceptance.

The Varieties of Legal Inquiry
and the Showdown Question

Law has many faces, and so there are many legitimate and useful inquiries that the scholar or student of law can pursue concerning any legal precept. One can study a precept's material causes, that is, the social forces and individual or group decisions that controlled or contributed to its making. Rewarding inquiries can be conducted, too, into such matters as the social legitimacy of the purposes the responsible lawmakers sought to achieve by enactment or adoption of the precept, or the meaning its terms are likely to bear for the judges and other officials to whose attention it will come in the future. If one is inclined to be something of a system-builder, as most card-carrying jurisprudents are, his principal concern may be to assign the precept at hand to its proper place in his jurisprudential scheme of things, and we can expect to see our precept characterized variously as "positive law," [1] "dynamic norm," [2] "primary rule of obligation," [3] or, more disparagingly, as mere "source of the law" [4] or "legal provision." [5]

There are many mansions in the house of jurisprudence, and I would not belittle anyone's perspective on law in society, provided only that he does not insist that his is the only perspective that gives a true or meaningful view of ultimate legal reality. Law is an intricate and crucially important social technology, and we must beware of the kind of dogmatic monism, not unknown in legal philosophy, that attempts to bring every aspect of law's functioning within a unitary scheme or explanation. The phenomenon of law in society is too complex to be compressed into a single analytical formula.

In this eclectic spirit and with the caveat just recorded, I suggest, for my part, that no discussion or appraisal of a legal precept is even substantially complete if it overlooks the threshold problem of the precept's efficacy as an influence on official and unofficial action. It will be a central thesis of these lectures that there is no more important question to ask about any statutory or case-law rule than this one: to what extent has this precept of law become a verifiable norm of social behavior?

Let us take as our first example the Civil Rights Act of 1964, hardly an earth-shaking enactment but one which has its significance as Congress' first substantial step in recent years towards joining company with the executive and judicial branches of the national government in the effort to eliminate, or lessen the rigors of, racially discriminatory behavior in the United States. Subsection 201 (a) of the 1964 Act, closely patterned on legislation adopted in a number of states many years ago, prescribes the following as a norm of federal law:

> All persons shall be entitled to the full and equal enjoyment of the goods, services, facilities, privileges, advantages, and accommodations of any place of public accommodation, as defined in this section, without discrimination or segregation on the grounds of race, color, religion, or national origin.[6]

Later provisions of the Act forbid the withholding or denial of the rights and privileges declared by the principal subsection and prohibit coercive interference with these rights and privileges, but the sanctions provided for enforcement of the Act are exclusively civil remedies. Violation of the Act's prohibitions is not made a federal crime. Instead, federal district courts are given jurisdiction to grant injunctions against racially discriminatory practices prohibited by the Act, and it is provided that injunctive relief may be sought by aggrieved persons and, in certain specified circumstances, by the Attorney General of the United States.

I have already spoken of the many useful inquiries that can be conducted concerning any legal precept, and the Civil Rights Act of 1964 is a good case in point. Like any statute of its general character, the Act can be many things to many people. It is, in one aspect, an intriguing case study in American constitutional law, particularly when read in the context of the discussions in committee between Attorney General Robert Kennedy and several senators on the question whether the constitutional basis of the Act should be put on the commerce clause, on Section 5 of the Fourteenth Amendment, or on both of these authorizations. This, we might say, is the special meaning of the Civil Rights Act of 1964 to a constitutional lawyer.

Another analyst of the same statute, working in the jurisprudential tradition of Roscoe Pound [7] and Learned Hand,[8] would see the struggle that led up to enactment of the Civil Rights Act of 1964 chiefly as a contest between competing social interests—the demand of Negro citizens for equality of treatment *vs.* the demand of the affected entrepreneurs and others allied in interest or attitude with them to be let alone to practice the older way of doing things—and would characterize the ultimate form of the statute, and particularly its exclusively injunctive sanctions, as a "balancing" or "compromise" or "accommodation" of the opposed interests. Still another scholar, looking at the Civil Rights Act of 1964 from the court-centered perspective that dominates much of American jurisprudence and legal scholarship generally, would take his lead from Holmes [9] and offer his predictions as to what the federal courts are likely "to do in fact" in Civil Rights Act cases, or, if he is a fact-skeptic of the Jerome Frank [10] school, would discuss the difficulties that will be encountered in securing reliable judicial fact-finding in this bitterly contested area of regulation.

But, even after all this, a showdown question persists. How efficacious has the Civil Rights Act of 1964 been, how efficacious will it become, as an influence on the behavior of the persons to whom its admonitions are addressed? To what extent are Negroes, as a matter of verifiable fact, experiencing "full and equal enjoyment" of the places to which they apply for accommodation— at sporting events and at the theater, in the East and in the South, in Class A hotels and in modest tourist courts?

A comprehensive investigation, along the lines just suggested, into the efficacy of the Civil Rights Act of 1964 would be far costlier than a library study of the court proceedings to date, far harder to plan, and vastly more difficult to execute. Yet what is there about the Act that we need more urgently to know, whether, pragmatically, as an empirical basis for possible future legislation in the same field of regulation or, more theoretically, as data bearing on some of our largely unverified assumptions about law's force as an instrument of social change? It can be, we know, a long and rocky road from "law in the books" to "law in action." [11] Some statutes and some case-law precepts—far more of both, I suspect, than we now realize—never make it and become, in Llewellyn's terms, "paper rules" [12] rather than "real rules" or, in Ehrlich's terms, "mere legal provisions" without corresponding social force in the "living law." [13]

The Efficacy of Law
as a Problem for Jurisprudence

The literature of jurisprudence maintains a sharp and proper distinction between the "validity" of a precept within a given legal system and its "efficacy" in the social order, and this line of distinction becomes blurred only when discussion turns to the marginal and rather antique issue whether statutes can lose their validity *qua* law, that is, be repealed, by desuetude. If we go by word count, questions of validity would seem to be vastly more significant than questions of efficacy in the universe of jurisprudence; for every sentence written about the considerations that condition the efficacy of legal norms there are at least a hundred addressed, in one way or another, to the ways and means of determining whether

9

a questioned norm is or is not to be considered a valid norm of the legal system.

Hans Kelsen, the greatest of the analytical jurisprudents, is perhaps the best case in point. He admits the idea of law's efficacy into his pure theory of law but only in a limited and somewhat grudging way: a particular norm is valid if the order to which it belongs is, on the whole, efficacious.[14] Once we have qualified the legal order as a generally efficacious one, questions of formal validity become central in Kelsenian theory and questions of efficacy of only peripheral concern. John Austin's emphasis, although in quite different terms, was much to the same effect. There is no sovereign in a society, and so no positive law, unless there is a discoverable habit of obedience by the bulk of the members of that society as to the generality of matters. But once that habit of obedience is found to exist, a sovereign command is positive law, whether or not actual behavior is in accordance with its mandate. And, to Austin, "the appropriate matter of jurisprudence" is positive law [15] and nothing, or not much, else.

Let me not seem ungrateful to my jurisprudential masters, the legal realists—at least not in the city where Leon Green and Karl Llewellyn did their greatest work. American legal realism does, to be sure, take us one good step forward on the way from the conventional province of jurisprudence to the world outside.

The insights into the realities of the judicial process furnished by Holmes, Cardozo, and the university-based legal realists are, above all, behavioral insights and tell us a very great deal about the efficacy of legal precepts as influences on the behavior of a limited but crucially important class of people, judges and specifically appellate judges.[16] It is manifest, too, that a legal precept's efficacy as a social norm can be affected profoundly by judicial rulings concerning it. There is nothing less efficacious than an unconstitutional statute, at least after the authoritative decision on its invalidity has been handed down, and we are all familiar with the many instances in which the social efficacy of a statute has been undermined by unduly restrictive judicial interpretations of its meaning or purpose.

What judges do with, and to, a legal precept is, however, only one of the factors which determine its efficacy as a behavioral norm. The frustrating experience that New York and other states are now having with legislation designed to bar strikes by teachers, sanitation men, and other public employees is quite sufficient evidence that a statute can be sustained in the courts against constitutional challenge, and sympathetically and favorably interpreted there, and yet fail utterly as a working norm of social behavior. What worries me about the long-standing preoccupation of American legal scholarship with the courts and what they do is that it may convey a false impression that the courts largely control the efficacy, as well as the validity and meaning, of legal precepts. Such an impression, if it prevails, is a more misleading "upper court myth" than the one Jerome Frank used to hammer away at,[17] for this version of the myth obscures the truth that the causes of a legal precept's efficacy or inefficacy are less likely to be found in the courtroom than in the world outside.

The Categories of Inefficacious Law

Writers on legal and political philosophy, when they address themselves to the problem of justice, have a way of approaching their problem by the back door, that is, by beginning not with an affirmative definition of the justice concept but with the notion or sentiment of *in*justice and the categories of official and unofficial behavior which, to the writer's mind, exhibit injustice in actual or potential operation. This is true even of St. Thomas Aquinas, a positive thinker if there ever was one, whose discussion of just and unjust human enactments proceeds, when it gets down to specifics, largely by enumeration and analysis of the kinds of unjust law: unjust with respect to the object (not for the common good), unjust with respect to the author (beyond the authority of the lawmaker), and unjust with respect to the form (imposition of unequal burdens).[18] Edmund Cahn's fine book, *The Sense of Injustice*,[19] embodies the same approach. Professor Cahn told me once that he began to write a book on the attributes of justice but became persuaded, as his thought developed, that the better path to an understanding of justice as a working process was by way of reflective exploration of the more accessible, because more widely experienced and felt, sense of *in*justice.

If this indirect approach works, as I think it does, in jurisprudential discussions of the problem of justice, perhaps it will do as well for our discussion of the problem of law's efficacy. So instead of attempting the presently impossible task of enumerating conditions and forces that will guarantee the efficacy of a legal precept, let us take a close look at some familiar failures of law and see whether there are meaningful categories of *in*efficacy into which some or all of these failures fall. Physicists and biochemists often say that scientific knowledge gains fully as much from experiments that invalidate research hypotheses as from experiments that verify them. Perhaps the same is true of law's experiments in the control of social behavior.

Legal precepts can fail to make the grade as working

norms of behavior, that is, as generally observed law, for many, many reasons. It is necessary, for general discussion, to arrange these experienced particular failures of law's efficacy into groups or categories, but I realize fully that this procedure exposes me to two dangers: first, to the risk of being charged with the common jurisprudential offense of needless invention of new terminology; and, second, to the risk of being understood as claiming completeness and precision for what is, at best, a partial and tentative classification. The risks will have to be assumed, for better or worse, because I can think of no other way to make the points I want to put before the house, as theses for discussion, in the first of these three Rosenthal Lectures.

I suggest, then, that at least five patterns or categories of inefficacy emerge plainly from a survey of various and sundry legal precepts, in all fields of legal regulation, which have remained "law in the books" and never quite or really made it as "law in action." Let us, at least provisionally, characterize these five categories of inefficacy as follows: (1) failures of communication; (2) failures to enlist supportive action; (3) failures to forestall avoidance; (4) failures of enforcement; and (5) failures of obligation. Doubtless there are other patterns of inefficacy that will appear to the discerning eye, but these five should be enough for the purposes of the present lectures.

Failures of Communication

Under the rubric, *failures of communication,* we can assemble the countless familiar and unfamiliar instances in which a statute or case-law rule fails as a behavioral norm because its mandate is not brought home to the people whose behavior it is supposed to influence. My favorite illustration of this category of inefficacy involves a high court judge who shall be nameless here but is renowned throughout his state and the rest of the country for his acumen and encyclopedic knowledge of the law. Driving along a country highway lined by signs proclaiming a speed limit of 45 miles per hour, our wise and upright judge accelerated to 55 miles an hour to pass a trailer truck and was at once hailed down by a highway patrolman. His honor, with friendly but somewhat condescending helpfulness, advised the officer, by statutory chapter and verse, of the existence of a special provision in the state's traffic code authorizing brief temporary speeds above the regular speed limit when a driver is overtaking another vehicle. The arresting officer expressed proper appreciation for this item of judicial knowledge but proceeded to tell our judge that the special overtaking provision of the traffic code had been repealed at the last session of the state legislature. I like this not too serious example of failure of communication, because the judicial hero—or victim—of the piece is, at once, one of the best informed and one of the most law-abiding of men. If anyone would have been alert to this change of law, it would have been he, and the new precept would have had full efficacy, as far as he was concerned, had he but known of it.

The case and statute law of contracts and commercial transactions is made up in large part of quite specific norms designed not only to provide a basis for the adjudication of disputes but also, and more importantly, to furnish rules of the road for the structuring and out-of-court adjustment of transactions. We are painfully aware, however, that many, perhaps most, of these rules are quite unknown or largely misunderstood by the constituency of businessmen and consumers to whom they are supposedly addressed. The most unscientific of amateur opinion polls will quickly disclose that practically everybody is sure that no oral contract is ever enforceable and believes, further, that a written agreement bearing the talismanic word "SEAL" or an impressive incantation of fictitious consideration is automatically enforceable to the letter, however unbargained-for or oppressive its terms may be. Legal institutions like the equity of redemption in real property transactions, the duty of a seller or landlord to mitigate damages, and the safeguards carefully written into statutes for the protection of consumer buyers in secured transactions are familiar learning to the lawyer, but the layman, if he knows of them at all, sees them through a glass and darkly.

The most painful reminder we have had in recent years of the extent of the law nobody knows is in the area of social security and, particularly, welfare legislation. Vitally important social interests are at stake here, and the relevant legislative and administrative directions are, by and large, fairly and carefully drafted to assure minimum standards of living and equality of treatment for those who have no other resources of their own. Yet reports from neighborhood law offices indicate that a full third of the social security and welfare clients applying to them were wholly unaware of their rights under existing federal, state, and local law. What better illustration could there be of the limited social efficacy, because of a failure in communication, of a carefully tailored and profoundly important legal program?

Earlier legal systems and legal theories put great emphasis on *promulgation* as an indispensable attribute of just law.[20] We do not take this classic requirement seriously enough, or imaginatively enough. It is a means both to the end of fairness in law's application and to the end of law's social efficacy. The quantity and variety of regulatory precepts that exist in our day cause us to chuckle ruefully at Bentham's old dream that a simple handbook might be distributed to all citizens, telling them everything they need to know about the law's possible impact on their personal and business affairs.[21] But this is no excuse for failing to use every effort to make legal provisions as intelligible as possible to laymen as well as to lawyers and to use all available resources of public information and education to communicate at least some knowledge of law's requirements and authorizations to citizens generally, and particularly to those for whom the advice of counsel is not readily available.

Here and there, during the past twenty-five years or so, developments have occurred that suggest possible lines of attack on the problems created for law's efficacy by what we have called failures of communication. These efforts, otherwise quite unrelated, have in common that they are all, in a sense, imaginative extensions of the idea of promulgation. An example comes to mind from my own carefully concealed past as a gang-buster. Late in 1942, the Office of Price Administration persuaded Professor David F. Cavers of the Harvard Law School to come to Washington to see what might be done to make OPA price regulations intelligible, particularly to the hundreds of thousands of small business men then poring over its edicts. I was then Director of Food

Enforcement for OPA, and I confess that I was quite uneasy about the simplification program. Our regulations were tightly drawn, with possible future enforcement litigation in mind, and I feared that the more simply written regulations, though more readily understandable to legally untrained businessmen, might be happier hunting ground for the discovery of loopholes and harder to make stick in the courts. Looking back on it now after a quarter of a century, I think I was right in my apprehensions; OPA's batting average in enforcement litigation, or so it was reported to me, was not as high after the simplification program as before it. But Professor Cavers and his sponsors were right in a far more important way. The Caverized price regulations, though somewhat harder to enforce in the courts, had far greater social efficacy, that is, far greater success as behavioral norms, than their more technical predecessors. Our illustration suggests an hypothesis that deserves investigation: understanding of the law's requirements is, at least on occasion, even more important than the imposition of coercive sanctions as an influence for widespread law observance.

We shall never be able to close law's communication gap altogether, but there are ways and means of narrowing it. Illustrations can be drawn from every field of law. Wider use of handbooks for jurymen, and substantial recent improvements in their quality, should contribute measurably to the efficacy of legal precepts as influences on the official behavior of these pro tempore adjudicative officers. In the field of consumer protection, there is a growing awareness among legislative draftsmen of the need to use direct and readily understandable language to get the legal message across to ordinary buyers. A good example is a recent New York statute [22] requiring that every retail installment sales contract include this express warning to the buyer: "Do not sign this agreement before you read it."

The insistence in recent Supreme Court decisions that accused persons be advised clearly and explicitly of their constitutional immunities and their right to counsel can be interpreted, I suggest, as another reflection of the idea that legal precepts cannot have efficacy as norms of behavior unless they are meaningfully communicated to the people favorably or unfavorably affected by them. Indeed, is it stretching the idea of promulgation too far to suggest that the vast new federal programs for the extension of free legal services are, in perhaps their most important aspect, efforts to increase law's social efficacy by narrowing the communication gap from lawmaker to law consumer? If we cannot give the ordinary citizen one of Bentham's "all you need to know" handbooks, we can through legal services reduce the incidence of law's failures of communication.

Failures To Enlist Supportive Action

Most precepts of the private law depend for support on private initiative; if claims are not presented or suits filed or defenses raised by the persons who stand to benefit from the application of a statutory or case-law rule, the rule is likely to remain a dead letter, both in the courts and in the larger society. The situation is different as concerns the precepts of the criminal law and of most regulatory legislation, since these are backed up by official enforcement action, but even here a statute may provide both for official sanctions, e.g., criminal prosecution, and unofficial sanctions, e.g., private suits for damages. In these and similar situations, where a legal precept's efficacy as a norm of behavior depends wholly or largely on private enforcement action, we are likely to encounter instances of a second type of inefficacy, which, for want of a better designation, we shall call *failures to enlist supportive action.*

Again I find my clearest illustration in the experience of that unique graduate school for law professors of my vintage, the Office of Price Administration. It was evident, when the Price Control Act was being drafted, that we would need the help of all the sanctions we could get, and we asked for three: criminal prosecution, injunction suit at the instance of the Price Administrator, and private treble damage action by any person from whom above-ceiling prices had been exacted. Sympathetic as he was to our plight, since he knew that we were facing up to a mass-production enforcement task of unprecedented proportions, the Attorney General of the United States was dubious about the proposed private treble damages sanction. It would, he feared, swamp both the federal district courts and the state courts and turn them into price courts rather than courts of general jurisdiction. We, for our part, argued earnestly that a mass sanction was needed for a massive enforcement job, that the price control regulations could not possibly be enforced without the enlistment of widespread private supportive action.

Finally, the Department of Justice and the congressional committees were persuaded, and the private treble damages sanction was enacted in the Price Control Act of 1942. And nothing whatever happened. The anticipated flood of private treble damages actions did not occur; there was not even a respectable trickle of them, beat the bushes as we did to find and encourage treble damages plaintiffs. Later the statute was amended to enable the Price Administrator to sue for three times the amount of the price overcharge if the purchaser declined to. This proved moderately useful but was, for obvious reasons, far less a contribution to the efficacy of the price control program than widespread private treble damages actions would have been. Even now I am not sure why the private treble damages section did not live up to our expectations for it. Were there fears of business reprisal against successful claimants, or did litigation seem too costly and too much trouble, or did a suit for three times the amount of an overcharge strike the average potential claimant as smacking of sharp practice? Whatever the explanation, it was not failure of communication; the availability of the treble damages action was advertised, although unavailingly, throughout the length and breadth of the land.

The story of private treble damages actions under the antitrust laws was much the same for many years, with hardly any suits and so with hardly any contribution to the efficacy of the antitrust laws, until, within the last decade or so, potential antitrust plaintiffs and their lawyers suddenly became aware that there might be "gold in them thar hills." [23] This experience, and experience with similar statutes, is reflected in the sanction provisions, already noted, of the Civil Rights Act of 1964, which authorizes injunction suits both by aggrieved private persons and, in specified circumstances, by the Attorney General of the United States. A most interesting study could be made of the incidence of private injunction litigation under the Civil Rights Act of 1964 [24] and, to the extent measurable, of the contribution of this litigation to the statute's efficacy as a working norm of social behavior.

The problem I have been describing as failure to enlist supportive action was stated even more broadly by Karl Llewellyn in an article written thirty-eight years ago:

> The ways of appellate courts in handling existing official rules presuppose the cracking of the toughest nut the statutory draftsman has to crack: the case is already in court; someone is already making an appeal to the official formula. Whereas one of the statutory draftsman's major problems is to look into existent behavior beforehand, to make sure that his formula, when it becomes an official rule, will not merely bask in the sun upon the books. He must so shape it as to *induce its application* . . . or else . . . his blow is spent in air.[25]

Llewellyn gave no illustrations, doubtless because he knew that every reader would think at once of a dozen or more. I think at once of the wills acts. There are important social interests in the passage of property by will, but a surprising percentage of people, including many of very substantial means, die intestate. Somehow the statute law in this area, whatever its other merits, is not so shaped "as to induce its application."

Problems in the enlistment of supportive action arise

fully as often in case-law as in statutory context. Illegal bargain cases furnish particularly good examples, because policy considerations ride high in this area of contract law, and courts decide cases with particular regard for the effects their rulings will have on subsequent social behavior. In one such case,[26] the Appellate Division of the Supreme Court of New York held that there was no right of compensation, either in contract or in quasi contract, for goods supplied to a buyer under an agreement procured by the seller through commercial bribery of the buyer's purchasing agent. The result in the case was justified explicitly on the ground that the fear of forfeiture would do more than anything else could to give efficacy to the state's laws against commercial bribery. Manifestly the effectiveness of this decision, as an indirect sanction of the commercial bribery laws, depends on the extent to which private supportive action has in fact been enlisted in the ensuing years, that is, on the incidence of litigated cases in which the defense has been raised and of informal settlements in which full payment has been resisted on the same essential ground.

In another case[27] the Court of Appeals of New York, by a sharply divided vote, decided that a race track gambler could recover his winnings from a bookie without deduction for sums he owed the bookie on unsucessful wagers. The policy issue, as framed by the prevailing and dissenting opinions, emerged as just about this: will the rule of the case do enough to discourage bookies to offset the encouragement it will give to horse players? Assuming, for the moment, that the majority of the Court had the better of the policy argument, the effectiveness of its ruling will depend on the extent to which it enlists supportive action. As far as I can discover, few plungers have sued, and few bookies have closed up shop, in the years since the case was decided. Perhaps the Court should have guessed that its ruling would not have great efficacy as a norm of race track behavior. Are we reminded, perhaps, of the many years during which the federal courts refused to exclude evidence secured by unlawful searches and seizures, suggesting—or just about suggesting—that the efficacy of the Fourth Amendment as a norm of official behavior might better be served by the institution of damage suits against police officers by criminal defendants?

Failures To Forestall Avoidance

The third of our categories of inefficacy, *failures to forestall avoidance*, requires less explanation than the preceding two, because the phenomenon common to all its instances is a familiar one to lawmakers, judges, and the practicing bar. Most legal precepts, as we have seen, are designed to influence behavior in society, either by prescribing what the lawmakers deem to be socially desirable ways of doing things or, and more often, by prohibiting what the lawmakers deem to be socially undesirable ways of doing things. To the extent that other ways of doing the same essential thing are not blocked off, the precept, whether directive or prohibitory in form, will be inefficacious as an influence on behavior.

The term "avoidance" has become a word of art in the literature of taxation, and it is in the tax area that the problem of forestalling avoidance has its clearest history and greatest current liveliness. The authors of a recent book on real property refer to the "tax avoidance gymnastics" [28] that brought about, and followed, the passage of such ancient enactments as *Quia Emptores* and the Statute of Uses. But the old acrobats were pikers by contemporary gymnastic standards. As the burdens of taxation have become heavier, many thousands of the ablest members of the American legal profession have become full-time or virtually full-time specialists in the task of lessening the impact of the tax laws on their clients' affairs, chiefly by suggesting and painstakingly working out alternative ways of accomplishing sought business or personal objectives. There is nothing unethical or socially blameworthy about this endeavor; indeed, we may wonder whether today's tax schedules would not be intolerable and economically destructive without

2 7

the moderating effect of contemporary tax avoidance techniques. But the lot of the tax legislative draftsman is not a happy one, since his statutory designs will have money-raising efficacy only to the extent that he can anticipate the endlessly varied possible counter-moves that private tax counsel may think of next.[29]

The problem of forestalling avoidance is not unique to tax law but exists across the board of legal regulation. Consider these examples, of hundreds that might be chosen. The New York state legislature held stubbornly for many years to the policy that adultery should be the only ground for divorce. But other ways of dissolution of marriage were not blocked off, and patterns of avoidance of the "law in the books" were quickly developed. Annulment became a more important institution of family law in New York than in any other state, and even greater recourse was had to the technique of migratory divorce. Whom New York had joined together, Reno and Las Vegas put asunder. The norm of New York law was divorce only for adultery, but the norm of social behavior became carefully engineered divorce by mutual consent, for those able to afford it.

Judge-made rules, too, can be deprived of or limited in their efficacy by what are, essentially, avoidance techniques. That encrusted landmark of our law of contracts, the pre-existing duty rule, has a sensible policy behind it: if a man has promised to do something for a fairly agreed price, he should be held to his bargain and not permitted to badger or blackmail the other party into agreeing to pay more. But there are many ways to skin a cat—and to get around the pre-existing duty rule—and most of us have concluded, rather sadly, that the rule has no efficacy at all as a control on the behavior of anyone who can hire a reasonably competent lawyer to draft a superseding agreement for him.[30]

I suspect—although there is no empirical evidence to verify or disprove my hypothesis—that something of the same kind happened to limit or offset the social efficacy of the many judicial decisions, extending over a century, in which the courts cut away the old idea of *caveat emptor* by extending the legal concept of implied warranty. The policy basis of this judicial development was clear enough: as a norm of commercial behavior, sellers of goods should stand behind the things they sell. Such facts as we have suggest, however, that progressive judicial expansion of the concept of implied warranty was accompanied, step by step, by wider use by sellers able to impose them of boiler-plate disclaimers of all warranties, express or implied. One cannot appraise the social efficacy of judicial decisions in this and similar fields of the case-law without taking into careful account the extent to which sought judicial policies may have been frustrated by failures, perhaps inevitable failures, to forestall avoidance.

Since the courts, in our tradition, operate on a piece-work basis, one case at a time, the avoidance problem is more elusive in the judicial process than in the legislative process. Legislative lawmakers, if they look at their problem broadly enough, can anticipate and make specific provision to forestall avoidance, but it is harder for the judge, even when he is persuaded in a case to strike down a challenged practice as socially undesirable, to formulate his *ratio decidendi* in terms that will prevent the use of other ways to do just about what the disapproved practice was designed to do.

Failures of Enforcement and of Obligation

We move now into the fourth of our categories of inefficacy, *failures of enforcement*. Enforcement, as I am using the term here, is the imposition of sanctions by or at the instance of some public prosecuting authority, and this takes us at once into more familiar jurisprudential ground. It is usual in jurisprudence to distinguish "law" from other influences on behavior on the ground that legal norms, and they alone, are backed up by the sanctions that politically organized society may impose on people who violate them. This is the line of distinction drawn by John Austin, to whom the sanction is the badge of a command of the positive law, by Holmes, with his emphasis on "the incidence of the public force," [31] and even, in a way, by Thomas Aquinas, who came near the imperative theory of law when he wrote that the discipline of human law is "the kind of training which compels through fear of punishment." [32] "Law," Hans Kelsen declares, "is a coercive order . . . the social technique which consists in bringing about the desired social conduct of men through the threat of a measure of coercion which is to be applied in case of contrary conduct." [33]

Coercion, the threat of sanctions, is, indeed, the distinctive means towards the end of law's efficacy, yet how little we know concerning its quantitative and qualitative effectiveness towards the sought end. It is seventy-one years since Holmes expressed his doubts in the despairing question: "Does punishment deter?" [34] Even if we break this question down into relatively more manageable components—that is, whom and in what circumstances and to what extent does the apprehension of punishment deter or not deter?—we have no real empirical data to go on. Perhaps the deterrent effect of enforced sanctions, even on specific classes of people and in specific sets of circumstances, is not measurable to any degree of accuracy at the existing state of development of the behavioral sciences. In any event, all we have now is guesswork, the informed impressions of able and experi-

enced lawyers and criminologists but guesswork none-
theless.

So I shall try some guesswork of my own. I have very
little professional expertise in matters of crime control
and criminal law administration, but I am rash enough to
venture three hypotheses bearing on the failures of law's
enforcement that bedevil our society. First, that Jeremy
Bentham hit the nail on the head when he insisted that
the *certainty* and *proximity* of a pain of punishment is
more important in the calculus of deterrence than its
intensity, that is, its severity.[35] To use a contemporary
illustration of this hypothesis, if a peddler of heroin to
juveniles faces and knows that he faces one chance in
three of a one-year jail sentence, that prospect is likely to
have a far greater deterrent influence on his behavior
than would be exerted on him by knowledge that he has
one chance in twenty of suffering a ten-year prison term
—or even the death penalty urged by certain excited but
not too analytical legislators. On this assumption, the
efficacy of the substantive precepts of the criminal law
depends far less on legislative decisions as to the sanctions
to be imposed for particular violations than on the prob-
ity, energy, and technical skill of the state's police and
prosecuting officials and on the investigative methods to
which they have recourse to apprehend law violators and
establish proof of their guilt. Threats of sanction have

little deterrent effect unless the threats are made good with reasonable frequency and regularity.

My second hypothesis is that the problems of law enforcement in contemporary society are basically quantitative problems, too few troops expected to do entirely too much work.[36] In our society, we are too ready to assume that almost every socially disapproved practice is an appropriate one to put under the ban of the criminal law. The question whether gambling or prostitution or the sale of marijuana or homosexual behavior between consenting adults should be made or kept a criminal offense is not only a philosophical issue of the extent to which the state should undertake to legislate morality.[37] It raises a further, and today perhaps more urgent, question of the extent to which efforts to give efficacy to these legal prohibitions require the diversion of desperately needed law enforcement personnel from tasks that are more central to the maintenance of the public peace and safety. The more criminal prohibitions we have, the thinner the resources of law enforcement have to be spread.[38]

A closely related problem is presented whenever, as often happens, fundamental changes in business practice multiply the occasions for unlawful behavior. The best case in point is shoplifting, which has increased many-fold in recent years as open-shelf methods have become dominant in retail marketing. This pattern of merchandising greatly reduces the number of retail clerks required and so the cost of doing retail business. At the same time, open-shelf marketing makes shoplifting more tempting to many susceptible people and, at least apparently, far easier to execute. Is the community under duty to assign many more law enforcement personnel than formerly to shoplifting violations, or is it arguable that the quantitative pressures on law enforcement have become so heavy that shoplifting losses have to be treated, for practical purposes, as essentially business expenses to be offset against a store's savings in salaries to sales employees? The problem is a vexing one in every city in the country, and law enforcement officials, faced with ever increasing demands on their resources, are not at all sure where the answer lies.

My third hypothesis, closely related to the one just examined, is that failures of law's enforcement are inextricably bound up with failures of law's obligation. The inner sanctions of moral obligation, feelings of fidelity to law, have, we suppose, even greater influence than coercive sanctions have on the law-observant behavior of most people. To the extent that obligation fails as a force for the efficacy of legal norms, coercive sanctions have to do it alone. If contemporary failures of enforcement are to be traced in large measure to quantitative pressures on the law enforcement system, a widespread decline in the feeling of obligation to law could make the quantitative burdens of law enforcement quite unsupportable.

So, after a long road, we reach the fifth of my categories of law's inefficacy, *failures of obligation.* It cannot be left out of the inventory, if we are to see the other four categories in anything like perspective, but the subject is complex and better discussed after we have taken stock of some of the other aspects of law's influence and efficacy. We shall be back to legal obligation and to law's failures of obligation in my third lecture, *Constitutionalism and Disobedience: The Law and Practice of Domestic Tranquility.*

II

Precepts and Consequences:

*The Uneven Correspondence
of Lawmaking Purpose and
Social Outcome*

THE PHILOSOPHER, Ernest Nagel, in his discussion of the methodological problems of the social sciences, has this to say:

> Planned actions rarely if ever take place in a social setting over which men have total mastery. The consequences that follow a deliberate choice of conduct are the products not simply of that conduct; they are also determined by various attendant circumstances . . . whose modes of operation are in any case not within complete effective control of those who have made that choice. Eli Whitney did not invent the cotton gin in order to strengthen a social system based on human slavery; Pasteur would have been horrified to learn that his researches on fermenta-

tion would become the theoretical basis for bacteriological warfare; and French support of the American revolutionary cause against England did not aim at founding a nation that would eventually make it difficult for France to continue as a colonial power in North America.[1]

Professor Nagel's words were not written specifically about lawmaking decisions and their consequences, but they might well have been. Statutes and case-law principles do not operate in social settings over which lawmakers have total mastery. In a sense, lawmakers propose, but society disposes; the ultimate outcome of a legislative intervention will often include important consequences that were unforeseen by the lawmakers and are entirely foreign to the original legislative purpose. The draftsmen of our tax laws did not aim at creating the expense account subculture of the 1950's or anticipate its marked effects in such remote areas as the economics, and so the seriousness and style, of the American theater. Those who formulated and those who now stand by the tort principle of liability only for fault did not anticipate, and perhaps do not yet appreciate, the effects of our model of personal injury litigation on the economics, the functioning, and the outlook of the American legal profession. The draftsmen of the Fifth and Fourteenth Amendments to the Constitution of the United States did not anticipate or aim at the insulation of corporate enterprise from state regulation which contributed as it did to the course American economic development took during the period from the 1880's to World War I.

This third illustration is particularly useful as it bears on the precise point I hope to make in today's lecture. I am not contending that the side-effects, the unanticipated consequences, of lawmaking decisions are always unfortunate. There are economists and economic historians who believe that the Fifth and Fourteenth Amendments, as applied by the Supreme Court in cases involving state regulation of corporate enterprise, provided indispensable conditions for the development of American industry during the last two decades of the nineteenth century and the first two decades of the twentieth, and so helped bring into existence the great industrial plant on which our contemporary affluence and our relatively generous social services are based. Be this as it may, the fact remains that the side-effect just considered was remote from the original purposes for which the Fifth and Fourteenth Amendments were adopted.

The Inevitable Side-effects
of Lawmaking Action

Lawmakers may, on occasion, build better than they know, which is another way of saying that the ultimate outcome of a legal intervention is sometimes more a matter of chance, that is, of good or bad luck, than a matter of legislative foresight. My guess is that the unanticipated side-effects of lawmaking action are more likely to be regrettable consequences than happy ones, but my point at the moment is the narrower and more jurisprudential one that the effects a legal precept will have in society may extend, by inexorable chain of causation, far beyond the scope of the original lawmaking design. A statute may or may not accomplish the objectives its makers sought to achieve when they enacted it, but these sought consequences may be outweighed and swamped in importance by the statute's unsought side-effects.

Why should this be so? The answer lies in part in the nature of the lawmaking enterprise. The problems with which law and lawmaking deal are complex social situations involving many variable factors. A legislative innovation is, in a sense, an experiment in the influencing of behavior but one that has to be carried on without controlled conditions. In a controlled experiment, a single new variable is introduced into a complex situation while the other factors in that situation are all kept constant. But there is no way of keeping the other behavioral variables constant when a new legal factor is introduced into a social situation, and the responses to the newly introduced factor can be many and various.

One response, considered earlier, may be the undermining of a statute's efficacy as a norm of behavior by the development of avoidance techniques. This, however, is but one of the possible responses to the stimulus of a new legal precept. In a true avoidance situation, a legal prohibition or a tax is circumvented by using another way to do essentially the same thing as would be accomplished by the legally prohibited or taxed course of action. The free and easy use of expense accounts can perhaps be characterized fairly as a form of tax avoidance, since essentially the same thing—that is, putting more spending money into the hands of a corporate employee—is accomplished as would be achieved by giving him a raise in salary on which he would have to pay taxes. But the existence of a legal precept may cause or encourage the people affected by it not merely to search for other ways of doing about the same thing but to do something quite different, e.g., switch from patent medicine manufacture to some less tightly regulated line of production, or transfer investments from metropolitan rental housing to suburban real estate, or make large contributions to institutions of private philanthropy or higher education. In short, the side-effects of a lawmaking decision include the consequences of law "avoidance" but include a great deal more besides.

Legal precepts, case-law and statutory, are not formulated in abstraction. The rules and principles declared by the appellate courts are, in a sense, by-products of the task of deciding particular cases. A thoughtful and sensitive court will be mindful of the consequences of a decision, as it may affect later cases and even the out-of-court behavior of certain classes of people, but the focus of the court's attention is on the case then before it and the type-situation that case represents.[2] A court working in the sound one-case-at-a-time tradition of the common law is unlikely to spend much thought on the remoter consequences of its decisions. When counsel offers unduly imaginative projections about undesirable side-effects a decision may have, the usual judicial reply is along the lines of "we will handle that problem if and when it arises in a case before us."

The legislative process, as it exists in fact, is hardly more abstract in character. Writing many years ago about our "piecemeal" approach to legislation, Harlan F. Stone complained that "we have legislated very much as we have declared law by judicial decision—to fit a particular case or particular types of cases." [3] So we have, and so we shall, I suspect, as long as our representative institutions retain their present nature and functions. The occasion for the enactment of legislation is typically a desire on the part of the legislators, often under strong pressure from constituents or from the executive, to attain certain particular objectives.[4] A legislature studying a specific proposal is like Eli Whitney at work on the mechanics of his cotton gin; both are concentrating on how to make a contraption work, and only incidental attention is given to the possible remoter consequences of the contraption's operation.

Procedural Reforms and Substantive Consequences

Reflective study of the social setting in which a proposed new legal rule or institution is to operate will often put the lawmakers on notice that certain unsought side-effects may result if the proposal is adopted, or adopted without specific safeguards against them. Sometimes, however, the side-effects are so surprising in nature that no one anticipates them, even though the rule or procedure involved undergoes long and careful advance study. This is true of the side-effects disclosed by recent empirical research into the operation of two widely discussed devices for improved judicial administration, split trials, and compulsory pretrial conferences.

Court congestion, with its intolerable delays in justice, is the most pressing problem of American law administration. Courts in every state are inundated by personal injury litigation, and years can pass between the filing of a claim for damages and its final disposition by litigation or settlement. Many proposals have been offered as partial remedies, one of them the split trial device in which a suit for damages is divided into two parts, the issue of liability and the issue of damages, and the liability issue tried separately and first. If the jury finds for the defendant on the issue of liability, that is the end of the case. The time required for the presentation of evidence on the usually complex issue of damages is thus saved in any case in which the jury finds for the defendant on the issue of liability, and the burden on the court reduced to this extent. The split trial procedure has been tried out, on an experimental basis, in the United States District Court for the Northern District of Illinois, and empirical analysis by Professor Hans Zeisel and others verifies the hypothesis that trying the liability issue first and separately does, in fact, accomplish an appreciable net saving in court time.[5] But a side-effect appears, a consequence not intended by the sponsors of the split trial procedure and quite foreign to their purpose. Use of the split trial procedure seems to bring about a striking increase in jury verdicts for the defendant. In personal injury actions generally, verdicts for the defendant are returned in approximately 40 percent of the cases; 40 percent to 42 percent is the standard and relatively constant figure. As against this, the verdict was for the defendant in 79 percent of the split-tried cases in the sample subjected to study.[6] The sought end of the split trial device, savings in court time, seems swamped in importance by the side-effect of the procedure in reducing plaintiffs' recoveries in personal injury litigation by almost one-half.

Comparable side-effects appeared when a carefully structured experiment with compulsory pretrial was carried on in New Jersey by my colleague, Maurice Rosenberg, and his associates of the Project for Effective Justice. The procedure of the pretrial conference was first proposed years ago as a means to the end of better courtroom presentation of cases, but, as court congestion became an increasingly grave problem, pretrial came to be thought of principally as a possible device for saving court time. The idea is, of course, that the pretrial conference may reduce demands on court time by making trials shorter and, more important, by encouraging out-of-court settlements. In the Rosenberg study, undertaken at the invitation of Chief Justice Weintraub of the Supreme Court of New Jersey, three thousand personal injury cases were examined.[7] In about three-fourths of these cases, pretrial conferences were held, either on a compulsory basis, by court order, or because a conference was requested by one or both of the parties. In the other one-fourth of the cases, there was no pretrial conference. Comparison of the pretried cases with those in the control group of cases never subjected to the pretrial procedure furnishes convincing evidence that pretrial is not effective as a remedy for court congestion. Actual trials were no shorter in the pretried group than in the control group, and there was no substantial increase in the percentage of settled cases.[8] The most interesting finding was that the pretrial institution has a substantive side-effect, not foreseen before by the judges, American Bar Association committees, and legal scholars who have urged compulsory pretrial as a reform measure, in that plaintiffs' average and median recoveries in the pretried cases were about 30 percent higher than in the cases that were not pretried.[9] There is a certain irony in this finding that pretrial tends to increase the amount recovered by successful claimants in personal injury actions, since defendants' lawyers, by and large, have been enthusiastic about compulsory pretrial while most plaintiffs' lawyers have been inclined to oppose it.

The unanticipated side-effects that seem to attend adoption of split trial and compulsory pretrial procedures are not the most dramatic illustrations on record of the uneven correspondence of lawmaking purpose and social outcome, but the illustrations are good ones to begin with, and for several reasons. The first reason is that the side-effects in our two judicial administration examples are not speculative; their occurrence is, to an extent at least, empirically verified. The technology of empirical research has been put to work here for appraisal of a legal institution's direct and indirect influence. It should be noted, too, that the side-effects of pretrial on the average and median amounts of claimants' recoveries might have escaped notice altogether if the research design had been less comprehensive and imaginative. If the Rosenberg inquiry had been only a time study, with no entries made of the amount of recoveries in pretried cases and other cases, we might be as ignorant now of the existence of the side-effect as we were before the study was undertaken. This suggests that empirical research into the operation of legal precepts and institutions can do more than verify or disprove the existence of already suspected side-effects; it can also, on occasion, disclose the existence of side-effects theretofore unsuspected. Anyone who has read Kalven and Zeisel's great book, *The American Jury*,[10] is struck by the way that study goes even beyond verification or disproof of the authors' original research hypotheses and suggests new and challenging dimensions for discussion of the jury system and for future inquiries into its operation.

There is one more point to get into the record before

we move from our discussion of the verifiable side-effects of split trials and pretrial conferences to other, broader and more speculative, illustrations of law's unanticipated influences. We would all agree, I am sure, that if there are to be substantial changes in the frequency of plaintiffs' recoveries in personal injury actions or in the average amounts received as compensation by successful claimants, these changes should be made on the basis of deliberate study and appraisal of the compensation system and not brought about as accidental by-products of changes in patterns of judicial administration. Lawmaking is an incompletely rational process to the extent that legal precepts and institutions brought into being to accomplish one purpose have significant social effects that are entirely foreign to that purpose.

"The Best Laid Plans . . ."

Instances of the uneven correspondence of precept and consequence, purpose and outcome, can be found across the board of law's operation. Is it true, as often charged, that the billions of dollars of federal money expended in the "urban renewal" programs of a decade or so ago had the effect of pressing many thousands of poor people into drastically narrowed enclaves of concentrated poverty? If that is true, the great probability is that the result was never intended or foreseen by those responsible for enactment of the legislation involved, but came about because of the operation of economic and social forces that had been incompletely analyzed when the program was planned. What of the familiar hypothesis, advanced by Thurman Arnold in *The Folklore of Capitalism*,[11] that the antitrust laws, in net effect, contributed more than just about anything else to the elimination of small business and the experienced domination of American industry by a relatively few giant corporations? Mr. Arnold later went on to be the devoted and effective Assistant Attorney General in charge of the Antitrust Division, but his conversion to the antitrust cause did not persuade everyone who had shared his original skepticism concerning the Sherman Act. A good many lawyers and scholars remain convinced that the norm of antitrust interpretation and enforcement that prevailed for many years, stricter application of the antitrust laws in loose-knit combination cases than in merger cases, made the antitrust laws a strong force for, rather than against, concentration of economic power in the United States. To the extent that this is true, we have an instance not merely of uneven correspondence of purpose and outcome but of their direct opposition.

Thoroughgoing and unbiased analysis of the operation of postwar rent control in New York City might disclose that the immediate consequences of the program are offset and perhaps outweighed by its side-effects. In suggesting this possibility, I may be what bankers and suburban ladies used to call Franklin D. Roosevelt, a traitor to my class. I was in favor of wartime rent control, participated in a small way in development of the design whereby rents were frozen at existing ceilings, and defended the constitutionality of that regulatory design in several court cases. New York's retention of a reduced but still substantial measure of rent control since the end of World War II may be a different story. The political explanation is clear enough—there are far more tenants than landlords—but what of economic and social justification?

There is little doubt about the substantial efficacy of the program as a norm of landlord and tenant behavior. Rent controls are well known and not very difficult to enforce, and the program has certainly enlisted its full share of private supportive action by tenants and tenants' associations. What, however, of the verifiable side-effects? There is reason to suspect that the retention of rent control has contributed appreciably to the deterioration of New York City's residential housing plant. Many landlords are sullenly reluctant to spend money, at 1968 labor and material rates, on the maintenance and repair of premises occupied at rentals related to standards that prevailed twenty-five years ago. Apartment properties formerly owned as sources of regular rental income have been transferred to land speculators, who hope to sell the sites at greatly increased prices and are not particularly interested in maintenance of the buildings now there. A distinct discrimination has set in in favor of older people, whose occupancy of rent-controlled apartments is likely to go back to the war years, and against the young. Older people do not move out of large rent-controlled apartments into more expensive smaller ones, and young families with children have to be squeezed into less commodious and far more costly new accommodations.

The developments just listed are items in an account. Do the immediate and manifest benefits of New York City's rent control program outweigh its complex and less visible disadvantages? A reasoned answer to this question would require both an inquiry into societal fact and a choice among conflicting social interests. I have deliberately chosen an illustration in which the commonly asserted side-effects of a legal institution are empirically verifiable, it would seem, but not yet verified. This would be research not merely into the efficacy of a legal prohibition as a behavioral norm but a good step farther into more elusive matters of unintended and indirect effect. It is plain, too, that our example is one in which evaluation of the regulatory program can be accomplished only by balancing its beneficial immediate results against its harmful remote consequences. One often encounters a weighing problem like this when he extends his analysis of an important legal precept from study of its immediate effects to inquiry into its possible wider reach as an influence on social behavior.

The Brooding Omnipresence of the Tax Laws

Taxation is the field in which legal scholarship is most sensitive to the more remote consequences of lawmaking decisions. The explanation of this unusual sensitivity may be that tax laws have long been used to accomplish non-revenue objectives. American political history is rich in examples: George III's tax on tea, Maryland's coercive tax on the Bank of the United States, use of federal tax power against child labor, license taxes on gamblers, and many many more. Today some tax scholars are fearful that "the integrity of the tax system" is being impaired by tax preferences designed to stimulate or reward private action deemed desirable by the lawmakers.[12] Awareness that many provisions of the tax law have and are intended to have non-revenue consequences makes the observer alert to the range and variety of the tax law's possible unintended social consequences.

If there is ever a sociology or jurisprudence of taxation, it will have as its subject matter the immense total impact of the tax laws on societies and their cultures. No reason appears why the parables of jurisprudence always have to be old and unlikely situations like the one involving the people in the lifeboat who had a youth for dinner,[13] and taxation furnishes uniquely instructive illustrations of law's direct and indirect influences on society. Tax considerations are often more important than any others in the structuring of transactions, the tactics of stock investment and speculation, the promotion of plays, even the making of financial arrangements for one's wife and family. Tax factors, like the poor, are always with us. I have one friend who moved his wedding date up from January to December for tax reasons and another who thought of postponing his from December to January, also for tax reasons. Professors are the least materialistic of men, and yet I know of a first-rate piece of scholarship that was written a full two years later than it might otherwise have been, because its author saw a high income year coming two years ahead and scheduled his uncompensated leave of absence accordingly. In contemporary American society, it is the tax lawmaker, not the piper, who most often calls the tune.

Jurisprudential writers like Ehrlich tend to see social institutions as arising spontaneously in society and social developments as phenomena largely uninfluenced by law.[14] This interpretation underrates law's force as a shaping influence on society and especially minimizes the force of tax law. There is a pretty well authenticated story about the Greek shipping magnate who was asked why he and his peers never make massive philanthropic gifts as American multimillionaires typically do. "We cannot afford to," he replied. "In America you save on taxes when you give to charities, but we are not subject to taxation and so would save nothing." This states the case too simply, but there is an element of truth in it.

A list of the remote and not so remote social responses to the stimuli of American tax law would include, as a few of its items, the growth of private pension plans, the complex market subculture of profit-taking, the increasing domination of American industry by conglomerates, the rise of the great foundations like Ford and of many smaller ones, and the unparalleled magnitude of American contributions to private charities and institutions of higher education. Tax considerations are not the only causative factor in these developments, but the tax factor is certainly a major contributing force and probably an indispensable one. This means that profound changes in basic institutions might be caused by simple amendments of the tax laws. If church property were made taxable and the tax deduction for gifts to churches abolished, the role of the churches in American life would have to be entirely recast. Similar changes in the tax position of private universities and colleges would inevitably bring about a virtual takeover of higher education by state-supported institutions.

More social institutions than we realize have been shaped by the tax laws and exist, in a sense, only at the mercy of the taxing power. One who would attempt the herculean task of appraising the contemporary American tax system will have to go far beyond matters that bear on the behavioral efficacy of the tax laws or on their efficiency as means to the end of raising revenue. There are indirect effects, some anticipated and even intended but others quite unforeseen, that are far too important to leave out of the account. The brooding omnipresence of the tax laws is perhaps the best reminder of all that the social outcome of a lawmaking decision can extend far beyond the range of the lawmaking purpose.

Draft Deferments and College Enrollments

If we need another illustration of how the reach of law's consequences often exceeds the lawmaker's purposed grasp, we can find it close to home, the total impact of the decisions that have been made from time to time with respect to student deferments from the draft. Some draft-related increase in college and graduate school enrollments must have been foreseen when the original decisions were made in this matter, but the decision-makers could hardly have anticipated and certainly did not aim at the staggering increases that actually came about. A college degree will soon be as common as a high school diploma used to be, and the draft exemption is clearly one of the major operating factors in the explosion of student enrollments. The development is probably irreversible; consider the cries of outrage from graduate schools and their administrators when a recent draft order threatened for a time to reduce graduate school enrollments below the numbers to which the graduate schools had very recently become accustomed. Vast new facilities have been created, the new community colleges and similar institutions, to accommodate hundreds of thousands of applicants who could not be taken care of at older colleges and universities and, for the most part, could not have met their admission standards. These new facilities would not be abandoned if the draft and the Vietnam war should end tomorrow. The first law of educational administration is that if seats are available students will somehow be found to occupy them.

The late Huey Pierce Long did very well with his slogan of "every man a king," and perhaps we shall decide, on balance, that the norm of every citizen a college graduate is a sound one for a democratic and prosperous society. My own sympathies run in this direction. But there are more items in the account than the makers of American draft policy have dreamed of. Cries of alarm are beginning to come through. Is a college experience meaningful for everybody, or are there those among the present enrollment, in new collegiate institutions and in old ones, for whom four years of college can be a harmful prolongation of adolescence? Are there dangers that the United States may soon face the tragic situation I saw this year in India, a vast over-supply of bookishly trained young people who cannot find employment of the kind they aspire to but cannot bring themselves to take blue-collar jobs? This source of explosive social tension has been felt in many European countries. Perhaps automation and the observable growth of service businesses will lessen its shock here, but it is not to be overlooked.

I have mentioned only a few of what can fairly be described as potential side-effects of student draft deferments. Many more could be listed, on one side of the ledger or the other, but we are not centrally concerned at the moment with the question whether the vast and probably irreversible rise in student enrollments is socially desirable or undesirable. I have used the development as still another example of the uneven correspondence of lawmaking purpose and social outcome. By their lawmaking decisions, the congressmen and executive officials who made the draft law what it is have probably exerted a greater influence on the future of higher education in the United States than all the university presidents and all the professors combined. The full operation of the draft laws, as of other laws, was not within the foresight and certainly not within the "complete effective control" of the men who made them. That is the central thesis of this lecture.

This discussion of legal precepts and their consequences was offered not to solve a problem but to identify one, for that is what jurisprudence is or should be about. Our problem is that law's influence on behavior and social institutions is quantitatively greater, far more complex, and even chancier than will appear to anyone who restricts his appraisal of legal rules to their sought effects. Legal precepts operate in society in a kind of open-ended way. The dynamics of society are such that a statute designed for one purpose may be a causative factor, or even the proximate cause, of far-reaching and largely unforeseen institutional developments. Something resembling the genetic fallacy [15] appears in legal evaluation when one supposes that study of the history and original motivating purpose of a statute can take the place of empirical analysis of its total impact on society. Inquiry of a more searching kind can lead the observer into thickets of unintended result and unanticipated consequence, but these thickets, too, are part and parcel of the province of jurisprudence.

Efficacy Research and Legal Evaluation

We have now reached the point in our discussion at which some stocktaking is in order. All lawmaking is a venture in social control. Every considered statute embodies a decision on the part of the legislators responsible for its enactment that a certain projected ordering of conduct will serve one or more sought social ends. Manifestly, these ends will be served only to the extent that the legally prescribed patterns of conduct achieve efficacy as norms of behavior, and, as we have seen, the behavioral responses of people to the stimulus of a legal precept may be quite different from the responses that precept was intended and expected to produce. In law, as elsewhere in life, things are easier said than done. Our five categories of inefficacy—failures of communication, failures to enlist supportive action, failures to forestall avoidance, failures of enforcement, and failures of obligation—warn of the pitfalls that may be encountered as a statute moves along the hard road from "law in the books" to "law in action." [16] And we have seen in this discussion that a legal ordering of conduct, whether or not it becomes an efficacious norm of what Ehrlich would call the "living law," may produce unsought and even unanticipated side-effects that have to be understood and appraised on their own merits.

Careful study in advance of the enactment or adoption of a new legal prescription, particularly of the full social setting in which the new precept is to operate, makes it possible to predict and make specific provision for some of the problems of efficacy that are certain to be encountered and some of the side-effects that the new precept may produce. Our principal shortcoming here is that we are not yet making anything like effective use, in legislative planning, of the knowledge and, even more important, the methods of inquiry of the developing behavioral sciences. Statutes that are designed and expected to influence important areas of interpersonal relations are often enacted without the slightest systematic study of the existing norms of behavior in those areas or of the probable effects the introduction of a new, legally prescribed, variable will have on a complex social situation. To do this is to shoot in the dark, and we shall continue to shoot in the dark until we have worked out institutional arrangements by which the insights and investigative methods of the behavioral sciences are utilized to narrow the inevitable margin of error of purposive lawmaking.

However careful and imaginative advance legislative research may be, the forecasting of a statute's probable efficacy as a behavioral norm will never be an exact science. We have abandoned old behavioristic notions that social responses to external stimuli fall within a relatively narrow range of possibilities. To quote Ernest Nagel again:

> Although the influence of men's beliefs and aspirations upon human history has been frequently underrated, it is equally easy to exaggerate the controlling force of deliberate choice in the determination of human events, even when the choice is based on considerable knowledge of social processes. It is a common experience of mankind that, despite carefully laid plans for realizing some end, the actions adopted result in entanglements that had not been foreseen and had certainly not been intended.[17]

If foresight concerning the probable future efficacy of a statute is inevitably limited, as we know it is, then hindsight must be brought to bear. More often than not, controlled empirical inquiry into a statute's efficacy becomes possible only after the statute has been on the books for a substantial period of time. Efficacy research, that is, close empirical study of the influence legal precepts are having on actual behavior in society, is what we need most for evaluation of the contemporary legal system, both its new regulatory precepts and its older, inherited, legislative and case-law rules.

Sustained inquiry into the efficacy of legal institutions

significantly advances our knowledge of law's role in society, and so qualifies fully as an end in itself, but it has its second aspect as an indispensable technology of law evaluation. It is unlikely, to be sure, that we shall soon be seeing a comprehensive program of efficacy research undertaken across the board of legal regulation. Serious inquiry along these lines is expensive, by legal research standards though not by standards that prevail in science, medicine, and other fields, and requires the working out of effective patterns of colleagueship between scholars of law and scholars of the behavioral sciences. Many topflight behavioral scientists are wary of such collaborations because they fear that the behavioral sciences may wind up as junior partners in the enterprise. There are those in the fraternity of legal scholarship who fear that inviting the behavioral scientists over into Macedonia to help us may, in one way or another, endanger the autonomy of the discipline of law and so the authority with which lawyers, judges, and legal scholars are accustomed to speak on law-related matters. These, however, are only transitional difficulties and tend to work themselves out when interdisciplinary research teams get down to practical work.

The more serious obstacles to the future of efficacy research relate to attitudes many people, and not lawyers alone, tend to have about already enacted law. There is a

tendency, particularly on the part of earnest law reform-
ers, to regard the passage of a regulatory statute as the
accomplishment of a mission and so to look ahead for
new injustices to conquer rather than back at the societal
consequences of what has already been enacted. Enthusi-
asm tends to wane once a long-sought proposal has made
it to the statute books. It seems sometimes that "Never
look back" is a slogan of law reform; few law improvement organizations have the staying power to keep with
a legislative reform until they have studied and verified
its efficacy as a behavioral norm.

There is another factor in this observable tendency to
regard an enacted statute as finished business. A precept,
once on the statute books, tends to take on a self-justify-
ing status. It is typically harder to repeal a familiar law
than it was to get it on the books in the first place.
Consider, for example, the quasi-constitutional position
that the workmen's compensation laws, the patent and
copyright laws, and the antitrust laws have come to
occupy in the thought of people who work with them.
There are vested interests, not least lawyers' interests, in
every section of these complex statutes, and who knows
what alterations in familiar ways of doing things might
be compelled if efficacy studies disclosed needs for dras-
tic statutory change? I clearly recall the bit of anguish
we all felt, even those of us who were all for adoption of

the Uniform Commercial Code, when the Code finally reached the statute books and made our N.I.L. and Uniform Sales Act expertise sadly obsolete.

I used to think when I was a young expert on legislation—now I am neither—that the ideal procedure for a fast-moving modern society would be to have all legislation enacted provisionally, that is, so drafted as to expire in three years or so unless renewed after searching re-examination of its practical consequences during the test period. I am persuaded now that general use of this procedure would create more problems than it would solve, but I wish that lawmakers and lawyers generally would think about statutes in something like these terms. After all, every statute is provisional in the sense that it can be sharply modified or even repealed if its inefficacy or social harmfulness is fairly demonstrable. Many states now engage in what has come to be called "continuous statutory revision," but these programs are designed merely to assure more orderly arrangement of statutory directions from one legislative term to the next. The needs of our own day require both an attitude towards the existing law that permits and insists on continuing checkup on even the best established of precepts and a comprehensive technology of efficacy research to make that attitude effective for continuing revitalization of the legal order.

III

Constitutionalism
and Disobedience:

The Law and Politics
of Domestic Tranquility

In the first of these three Rosenthal Lectures, I advanced the hardly debatable proposition that a constitutional, statutory, or case-law precept has *efficacy* in a society to the extent that the actual behavior of the people who compose that society, both officials and the generality of private citizens, conforms to the standards which the precept directs or authorizes. Today we address our attention to the social phenomenon, or political ideal, that we call "the rule of law." The showdown question is again the question of efficacy. The rule of law exists in a society only to the extent that the actual behavior of people, both the society's officials and its private citizens, conforms to the standards prescribed by its laws.

The Neglected Aspect of the Rule of Law

The law's imperatives run both to a society's officials and to its private citizens. The police power of politically organized society can, in a sense, be likened to a firearm. A gun is a morally neutral instrument; one can use it to commit a crime or to protect his family from violence. Similarly, the state is inherently and unavoidably an ambiguous institution, at once a potential invader of individual interests and expectations and the protector of these interests and expectations against impairment by vicious or wayward private persons and groups. A lawless state, we know, can do profound wrong to individual aspirations and security. Private violence, when uncurbed by state power, can work in an equally dreadful way. Murder can come about by a railroaded conviction in court or star chamber, or at the hands of a lynching party. A printing press can be wrecked by state-supported storm troopers or burned, as Garrison's was, by a private mob. Property can be seized unjustly by agents of state power or confiscated by private looters. A speaker's right of free expression is equally destroyed whether he be arrested by a sheriff or howled down by private dissidents who do not want him to be heard.

A political philosophy is lopsided and authoritarian, we feel, if it interprets the rule or supremacy of law exclusively or chiefly in terms of the control laws exert on the behavior of private citizens. This is the ground on which we in the Western countries have been critical of the ideas of "socialist legality" that dominate jurisprudential discussion in the Soviet Union and the countries most closely associated with it. But a political philosophy is equally one-eyed if it sees constitutionalism—the rule or supremacy of law—chiefly as a matter of law's controls over official behavior and fails to give equal emphasis to law's task of control over the behavior of the society's citizenry.

The Anglo-American legal and political tradition exhibits far greater concern about possible official misconduct than about the dangers of private lawlessness. This emphasis in our political philosophy is, I think, deeply rooted in the historical experience of many centuries ago. A strong central government was established far earlier in England than in the countries of the continent of Europe. In times when the inhabitants of France, Italy, and Germany were longing for the emergence of a central political authority strong enough to protect them from lawless feudal nobles and warrior bands, royal authority already had effective power throughout England, and highly placed Englishmen were beginning to devise ways and means to keep the royal power within constitutional bounds.[1]

The British colonists in what became the United States brought the English constitutional tradition with them, and frequent collisions of American interests and aspirations with the designs of remote rulers in London tended to make American political intellectuals even more distrustful of centralized power and even more determined to establish institutional checks on its exercise. Otis and the Adamses in New England, and Henry, Jefferson, and Madison in Virginia, were not rebels against the English constitutional tradition; in their preoccupations and their principles they were more English than the English of their day. Accordingly, the prohibitions of the American Bill of Rights, like the British constitutional models on which they were patterned, run against official power-holders. Nowhere in the world are the essential civil liberties safeguarded more effectively against possible state oppression. We Americans are shocked to the depths of our being when officials act violently and lawlessly—and well we should be.

Understandably, the same emphasis characterizes our political theory. When an American or an Englishman writes or speaks about the rule of law or the supremacy of law, he means chiefly law's rule or supremacy over what public officials can and cannot do. Consider, for example, this quotation from the remarks of Judge Charles Wyzanski at the 1955 Harvard conference on *Government Under Law:*

> All that one seems able to spell out of the rule of law concept, when looked at universally, is, first, that the state recognizes a presumption that an individual has the right to have his person or property *free from interference by any officer of the government* unless that officer can justify his interference by reference to a general law, and second, that the state provides some machinery for the vindication of that right before an independent tribunal. . . .[2]

The italics are added; Judge Wyzanski has spelled out of our tradition precisely the emphasis that is there.

The same one-sidedness in interpretation of the rule of law idea appears in more exaggerated form, *mea culpa*, in the following:

> The one nugget of agreement discernible in the American writings is the idea, with which I devoutly agree, that state power is the great antagonist against which the rule of law must forever be addressed. The notion of an imposed or self-accepted constraint on governmental power may not exhaust the concept of the rule of law, but there is substantial agreement in

American thought that the rule of law's great purpose
is protection of the individual against the state.[3]

This comes close to saying, as I reread it now after ten
years, that we do not have to worry too much about
private group interference with civil liberties and social
regularity if public power-holders are kept under effective rein. Such might be acceptable doctrine for a community of saints, but not for contemporary society. To
say this is not to suggest that we should think less than
we do about law's role as a constraint on officialdom. My
point is simply that we should give equal time in our
reflections to law's necessary constraints on the liberty-
infringing behavior of society's rank and file. These constraints, too, are means to the end of human freedom.
Constitutionalism abhors anarchy equally with tyranny.

A scholarly minded observer from outer space, reading English and American political documents and commentaries for the first time, would quickly draw the
inference that Englishmen and Americans, as a matter of
history, must always have been far more law-abiding
than their governors. Be that as it may, it is time now to
see both aspects of the rule of law. The common good
can be as much endangered in a society by the excesses
of private lawlessness as by the oppressions of public
power. We turn then, with greater concern than formerly, to the ways and means of law's governance over

the generality of citizens. If you hear a rasping whisper from the back row, that is the ghost of Thomas Hobbes, telling us that he and John Austin and Holmes knew all along that they had hold of the right problem, whatever we may think of their solutions to it.

The Composite Forces of Law Observance

We have taken law observance too much for granted. When one thinks about it, it is an astonishing phenomenon—fully as remarkable as anything in the wonderland of present-day physics—that two hundred million people of widely varying interests, temperaments, and inclinations will, by and large, conform their conduct to precepts as detailed, intrusive, and inconvenient as those of contemporary American law.[4] To use but one example, the extent to which people pay their income taxes in the United States and the United Kingdom is a downright miracle, whether judged a priori or by comparison with norms of tax evasion that prevail in other countries fully as civilized as ours.

We are apprehensive these days about crime and civil disorder, and we turn to the reports of the President's Commission on Law Enforcement [5] and the National Advisory Commission on Civil Disorders [6] to find out how such things can be. We have been caught up short in our assumption that prevailing law observance is a natural order of social being, and we are surprised and fearful to have that assumption shaken. But the most surprising thing is not that laws are sometimes or often violated but that they are conformed to by the bulk of people as faithfully as they are. The legal control system is a complex mechanism, and it may be more fragile than we have supposed it to be. The sound procedure, however, is to look first at how the legal control system works, when it works, before we turn to the instances and causes of its failures.

Men conform their behavior to law partly from fear of law's coercive sanctions and partly from feelings of obligation. The term "obligation," as I am using it, has a broad meaning and includes not only conscious and thought-out ethical decisions that one's behavior in a situation should conform to law's requirements but also the undeliberated choices of law-abiding behavior that people make without really considering illegal alternatives. In any society in which the rule of law has reasonable efficacy, sentiments of respect for law are so deeply ingrained that in most matters it does not even occur to most people to act other than as law's rules prescribe. This, I think, is what Thomas Aquinas meant when he wrote of a "custom" of law-abiding behavior "that avails much for the observance of laws." [7] Whatever the merits may be in the long-standing jurisprudential debate concerning the relations of law and morality, the imperatives of the legal order carry at least prima facie rightness to most members of the community. To the ordinary citizen at least, the law does indeed, as Blackstone put it, command what is right and prohibit what is wrong.[8]

Philosophers have differed for centuries as to the relative force of the inner sanction of obligation and the law's external sanctions as causes of law-observant behavior, but there is no disagreement that the compound, in one proportion or another, makes law tolerably effective and social order possible. The relative contributions are unmeasurable. You may take the view that coercive sanctions are the stronger causative force and I that obligation is the stronger force, but these are impressions and surely not verifiable scientifically. One who would essay the comparative measurement would encounter too many qualifying variables: factors of time and place, variations from person to person and group to group, differences in the social persuasiveness of this law and that law, and many more. The most we can say at the present state of our knowledge is that feelings of obligation and fears of sanction are composite forces which, working simultaneously and in tandem, bring about the supremacy of law. Whether one force could ever do it without the other, no man can say.

One must be careful, in discussions like this, not to

think of obligation and coercive sanction as if they were entirely separate forces without influence on each other. If I have a guess concerning the generality of people, it is that they tend to feel far less obligation for unenforced legal imperatives, particularly when they see other people "getting away with it." If this is true, effective law enforcement is not to be underrated as a form of community moral education. Community awareness that sanctions are being imposed promptly and regularly for violations of law strengthens, except in the most unusual of circumstances, the feelings of legal obligation that prevail in that community. People are inclined to believe that what the law requires is probably right, and the fact that sanctions have been imposed on violators of a law is typically regarded as strong further proof of that law's rightness. This hypothesis is, I believe, verifiable empirically if someone could be persuaded to undertake it. Nor should we neglect the corollary proposition that failures of enforcement can bring about widespread failures of obligation.

Obligation and Its Failures

Our generalization, shortly stated, stands about like this: most people obey most of the law most of the time either because they feel in their hearts that they should, or because they are apprehensive of possible punishment if they do not, or for both these reasons at once. "Most people," I said, because in any society, however law-abiding, there are those whose psychic constitutions are such that they are deterred from illegal behavior only by the fear of apprehension and punishment. We can and do study the predisposing causes, hereditary, environmental, and accidental, that have made these people strangers to the idea of legal obligation, but, taking them as they are, the conventional technology of coercive law enforcement is the only available means of influencing their behavior. That technology is all society has for dealing with the hard core, whatever their number may be, who are outlaws by basic temperament and inclination.

So there is never an end to the game of cops and robbers. Society, in self-defense and in fairness to its law enforcement representatives, must do better than it has in the past to provide the men and matériel required for effective enforcement of the criminal law. If legislators and executive officers were as grudging in appropriations for the space program as they have been in appropriations for the police, the astronauts would not yet have been much higher in the atmosphere than the top of the Tribune Tower. Even the courts should be more mindful than they sometimes seem to have been that issues of what is due process in criminal procedure, however neatly framed in constitutional law terms, are not simply civil liberties questions of man against the state but may also be subtle problems in the balancing of conflicting social interests.[9] To say this is not to prejudge the issues at hand but to see another urgent dimension of the problem.

Some of the best minds in American law and law-related social disciplines are groping for ways and means to answer what the President's Commission on Law Enforcement and Administration of Justice describes, somewhat grandiloquently, as *The Challenge of Crime in a Free Society*.[10] Yet we know that crime, on however reduced a scale, would remain a phenomenon of social life even if criminal law enforcement were 100 percent effective, that is, even if every criminal act were followed inevitably and promptly by apprehension and punishment of the offender. Some unhappy people are driven by impulses stronger than the fear of even certain punishment. Others, even more unkindly endowed by nature, are dominated by passions of self-destruction that make them create occasions of punishment rather than avoid them. Law's technology of deterrence is largely meaningless for them. Law's coercive techniques, like law's substantive precepts, have to be designed for general application. Most people, in any event, are not beyond the influence of law's coercive sanctions. Nor are most people insensitive to the promptings of legal obligation.

It would be wonderfully convenient, for lecturers on jurisprudence as well as for police officers, if all the inhabitants of the social world could be divided into two mutually exclusive categories, the utterly criminal in one group and the perfectly law-abiding in the other. Yet we know that human personalities cannot so readily be classified as either sheep or goats. The force of legal obligation will differ from man to man, from Al Capone, say, at one end of the continuum of civic virtue to your colleague, Nat Nathanson, or my colleague, Elliott Cheatham, at the other. For the generality of people who occupy points somewhere along the continuum, the abstract and universal idea of fidelity to all laws all the time has more appeal in theory than in practice. Just as there are banks robbers who obey traffic laws and burglars who pay their debts, most ordinarily law-abiding people exhibit a kind of selective legal obligation, faithfully observing the requirements of most laws but playing fast and loose with others.

Thomas Aquinas wrote that just human laws have the power of binding in conscience, whereas unjust laws are not so binding, "except perhaps in order to avoid scandal or disturbance." [11] Social behavior evidences much the same kind of discrimination. By and large, people are most strongly motivated to obey laws they consider fair and sensible. If the law's requirements fail to come through as sensible, one who doubts the good sense of the legal requirement is likely to feel far less obligation to abide by it. One of the first drinks of bourbon whiskey I ever had I enjoyed in 1932 in the study of a federal judge, who was scrupulous and severe in holding himself and other people to strict observance of all the laws except Congressman Volstead's. The prevailing attitude, to which I have earlier referred, that what the law requires is probably the ethically right thing to do is not an irrebuttable presumption, particularly not when a man finds his customary and agreeable habits of behavior interfered with by what he considers trivial and unreasonable enactments. If I had been so ungrateful as to ask my judge-host of thirty-six years ago how he reconciled his disregard of the prohibition law with his general habit of obedience to legal imperatives, he might well have answered with a variation of *de minimis non curat lex;* the law should not concern itself with such trifles, and, when it does, normal legal obligation does not attach to trifling precepts.

It is always risky business to draw comparisons between the deeply felt present and the indistinctly remembered past, but one senses, in these days, a widespread attitude of mind in which rules, and not only legal rules, are thought of as less authoritative and less obligatory than they seemed formerly. Regulations once taken for granted and conformed to more or less cheerfully and habitually have come to be viewed in a more critical way. It is as if the burden of proof has been shifted from where it used to be, on the person trying to justify his disregard of an established rule, to the rule itself. This more critical, almost cavalier, attitude towards authority and authoritative rules generally carries over as concerns the obligation of legal rules, and this particularly when obedience to law would be against individual or group interest.

In New York City, the new era of skepticism towards the rules of the social game and the authority behind them was perhaps best symbolized when the late Michael Quill of the Transport Workers Union, an amiable and engaging man in most ways, appeared on television during one of the worst of the city's subway strikes and broadcast his defiance of law by tearing to bits a court injunction issued that day against him. The same explicit rejection of the authority of statutes and court orders has now been recorded by New York's school teachers and sanitation employees and threatened even by firemen and policemen. To be sure, striking public employees and their leaders invariably assert their general fidelity to law and use some form of the familiar rhetoric that the particular statute or court order they are defying is unjust and therefore not valid law at all. But, as always, men tend to define the just and the unjust in their own terms and with their own interests in mind. The frustrations that New York and other cities are having with illegal strikes by public employees are, in one aspect, *failures of enforcement*, since technical legal problems of sanctions and the tactical use of sanctions are centrally involved. But the underlying cause, which makes the problem of sanctions as hopeless as it seems at the moment, is a *failure of obligation*.

In other even more troubled areas of the social system, law violation and disorder reflect the existence of deep resentments against the entire legal, political, and economic situation in which the law violators find themselves. Let me underline here a central thesis of this discussion. The attitude we call legal obligation does not arise from attachment to distinctively legal processes and institutions. Fidelity to law, or infidelity to law, is inseparable from one's feelings about the total social and political order of which law is but a part. If a society is wanting or seems to be wanting in the quality of distributive justice, or if substantial groups of citizens are excluded from participation in its essential political and social processes, obligation to law will not exist among the underprivileged and disaffected in that society, however just and efficient its judicial and other purely legal processes may be.

The feelings of legal obligation that prevailed long and distinctively in the United Kingdom were not merely expressions of confidence in the workings of the British legal system; they were expressions of at least reasonable satisfaction with the entirety of the British political and social order. When we examine the conditions and factors of legal obligation, law and politics are inseparable. Domestic tranquility is maintained not by law alone but by fairness and justice in the working of political and other social processes. In the words of the President's Commission on Law Enforcement and Administration of Justice:

> . . . no system, however well staffed and organized, no level of material well being for all, will rid a society of crime if there is not a widespread ethical motivation, and a widespread belief that by and large the government and the social order deserve credence, respect and loyalty.[12]

The causes of crime and civil disorder, in large part, can lie deep in resentments against society as a whole and particularly in impressions of social injustice. The draftsmen of the Constitution of the United States may have sensed this when they framed the Preamble to the Constitution in such a way that the stated purpose, "to establish justice," accompanies, and indeed precedes, the stated purpose, "to insure domestic tranquility." Domestic tranquility without social justice is the precarious quiet of repressive power, coercive sanctions keeping the peace unaided. Enduring order comes to a society only when the norms established by that society's laws and customs are—and are seen to be—tolerably just to all the vital and self-conscious elements of which that society is composed.[13] I say "tolerably" just, because that is all any of us can ever expect from imperfect human institutions; perfect social justice is an idea in the mind of God and not to be found or hoped for in the city of man. But this concession detracts not at all from my central point, which is that justice and domestic tranquility are everywhere as inseparably linked as in the great Preamble of 1789.

We are asking too much of our forces of public control—that is, of our only too human police officers, courts, and agencies of law enforcement and social mediation—if we expect them to maintain order, compel the conditions of public peace, unless the norms prescribed by law and social practice are considered tolerably fair and just by the overwhelming generality of citizens. Nor is it enough that a majority be reasonably content with legal and social norms as they are; social assent requires a broader base than 51 percent, or even 80 percent, acquiescence. In our form of social and political organization, minorities are supposed to yield, in most matters, to the majority will. But democratic government is headed for trouble whenever majorities insist on having everything their own way, however strongly held the minority interest and aspiration may be. "One man, one vote" is an acceptable standard for judging the constitutional validity of legislative districting. But a prudent majority will recognize that there are great issues on which one man's profound conviction and commitment should count far more than another man's mere preference to the contrary.

Law, Disorder, and Social Reform:
Short-Term Costs and Long-Term Gains

The most widely discussed finding in the *Report of the National Advisory Commission on Civil Disorders* is stated by the Commission in these bitter terms:

> White racism is essentially responsible for the explosive mixture which has been accumulating in our cities since the end of World War II.[14]

In this view, the incidents and agitations that touched off the 1965 riot in Watts and the 1967 riots in Newark, Detroit, and many other cities were but the occasions of the tragedy; racial injustice was its proximate cause. And when the Kerner Commission moves in its report from "Why did it happen?" to "What can be done to prevent it from happening again?" it suggests a comprehensive program to overcome the impediments that "white racism" has kept in the way of the attainment of genuine racial equality, social and economic as well as legal and political.

"White racism" is rather more a slogan than an analytical concept, but no one could agree more than I do with the Advisory Commission's finding that racial injustice is, historically, the proximate cause of contemporary racial disorder and with the Commission's implicit prediction that we shall not see the end of civil disorder in the United States until we have put an end to racial inequality. That view is entirely right as a long-term proposition, so there is every reason to get a basic program of social correction under way at the first possible moment. It does not follow, however—and we shall be grieved and disappointed if we think it does—that, as a short-term proposition, civil disorders will decrease in frequency and asperity in proportion to the accomplished decrease in racial inequality. There is a dangerous oversimplification here, and students of contemporary society are in need of warning against it.

One of the wisest of the world's social scientists, Robert I. MacIver, has recorded this highly relevant observation:

> One thing that struck me was a direct relation between the degree of liberation of groups and peoples from powerlessness or sheer subjection and the amount of social violence and civil commotion. In other words, liberty in this context brought forth not peace but the sword. In the longer historical perspective, there have occurred successive waves of social liberation, elevating subject classes from elite domination, abolishing slave classes, turning serfs into free workers or owners of land, raising workers from utter dependence on exploiting employers to membership in masterful unions, abolishing colonialism over the undeveloped areas of Asia and Africa and Latin-America, extending the right to vote to the very poor, emancipating women from legal and social subservience, asserting the rights of disprivileged minorities to equality of opportunity. Not only did this gradual process of liberation increase the amount of civil strife and social violence; it also, in our own age, the period in which these movements have been most fully advanced, culminated in the bloodiest holocausts of war in human history.[15]

Arthur Vanderbilt used to say that improvement of the administration of justice is no sport for the short-winded. Similarly, the achievement of racial equality is no task for the short-winded—or the short-tempered. Our planning for the next decade will be off center if we expect civil disorder to decline progressively as gains are made, step by step as they have to be made, against the underlying causes of racial injustice. The ratio of equality to disorder is likely to run quite the other way, as the Advisory Commission itself suggests in the section of its report entitled "Revolution of Rising Expectations":

> Ironically, it was the very successes in the legislatures and the courts that, more perhaps than any other single factor, led to intensified Negro expectations and resulting dissatisfaction with the limitations of legal and legislative programs. Increasing Negro impatience accounted for the rising tempo of nonviolent direct action in the late 1950's, culminating in the student sit-ins of 1960 and the inauguration of what is popularly known as the "Civil Rights Revolution" or the "Negro Revolt." [16]

The MacIver hypothesis that social liberation is accomplished only at the cost, at least the short-term cost, of increasing public disorder and violence, has profound political and jurisprudential implications. If the policies and programs urged by the National Advisory Commission on Civil Disorders are to be adopted by the government of the United States, let them be adopted on their merits, as long overdue rectification of America's historic injustice to its Negro citizens, and not as concessions made to quiet Black America down. If MacIver's hypothesis is sound, and I strongly suspect that it is, only disappointment is ahead for any expectation that relative improvement in the economic and social situation of most American Negroes will at once cause them and their leadership to be more "moderate" in their demands or less abrasive and disruptive in their tactics of social action. Things do not work that way, and the package of racial justice should not be sold with false representations. If it is so sold, we shall underestimate the social frictions ahead for our next ten years or so, and disappointed expectations can lead to despair and social reaction on the part of a disappointed majority.

Here, I suggest, is an insight that must be brought to bear in jurisprudential discussions of law and social change. One of law's highest tasks is the eradication of social injustices which, however long imposed by legal sanctions or private oppression, may some day undermine the public peace and order. Yet as progress is made, step by step, towards this objective, the pressures on the legal control system are likely to mount rather than decline. It is a curious idea that the prevalence of disorder may be the best measure of a society's progress towards social justice, but perhaps there is consolation in it for our troubled times.

And, Lastly, of Civil Disobedience

It is a relatively short step from what we have just been talking about, law violation and civil disorder as reflections of deeply felt grievances against the entire social structure, to the final theme I want to touch on in these lectures, the political and social tactic of civil disobedience. Neither of our "composite forces," neither obligation nor fear of sanctions, moves the practitioner of civil disobedience. In conscience he feels, or asserts that he feels, no obligation to the law he disobeys. To him it may be a pernicious and unjust order or enactment; in any event he has or proclaims a higher law or more urgent social value to which he owes fidelity. Nor is he deterred by the law's external sanction. If it is visited on him, that is the price he has declared himself willing to pay. Indeed, if he is of the older breed of law resisters, he may welcome imprisonment as a means of publicizing his cause in the tried and proven way of martyrdom. Civil disobedients of the newer model are considerably less enthusiastic about the acceptance of punishment as a form of witness to society—and tend to become remarkably legalistic when their day in court comes—but perfect consistency is no more to be expected from social dissidents than from pillars of the Establishment.

In past discussions of this theme,[17] I have attempted to distinguish revolution from civil disobedience on the ground that the revolutionary wants to bring down a whole social and political order and put another in its place, whereas the advocate of civil disobedience is aiming his fire at a particular set of laws or social institutions in a society otherwise tolerable to him.[18] I have now concluded that this distinction takes us nowhere. It is far more difficult than it used to be to draw a hard and fast line of distinction between revolutionary action and civilly disobedient action. How, for example, would we classify the leadership of the Black Panthers or the self-proclaimed "revolutionists" at the head of the SDS? Again, perhaps, the best way to approach the problem is to think in terms of a continuum ranging from the avowed and effective revolutionary, at one end, to the nonrevolutionary social reformer at the other. This century's two greatest strategists of civil disobedience can, I think, be located at the two ends of the continuum. Mahatma Gandhi's avowed and accomplished purpose was revolutionary, not to improve the quality of British rule in India but to overthrow it. Martin Luther King sought, and to an extent achieved, not the overthrow of the American constitutional order but an improvement in the quality of American culture.

Fifteen or twenty years ago, it would not have occurred to a Rosenthal Lecturer to include civil disobedience as a theme for jurisprudential discussion. To be sure, there would have been a vast literature to draw on, exemplified by the Antigone of Sophocles and by John Locke's "appeal to history" as recorded in our great Declaration of 1776. We would all have been mindful, too, of abolitionist defiance of the Fugitive Slave Law, of the tea in Boston Harbor, and of Thoreau in Concord Jail. But would all this have been "relevant," as the contemporary student idiom puts it, to the problems of our country and our time?

You and I would have thought not, I suggest, and we would have recited the credo of American constitutionalism. Let us consider, for a moment, what constitutionalism means. This society is, in its aspiration at least, a representative democracy based on the principle that laws are best made, and changed, by representatives elected by the people to the federal Congress and the state legislatures. It follows, according to this constitutional model, that social controversies, conflicting social interests, are resolved at the ballot box and not by general strikes, disruptive protest, or other extraconstitutional pressures. It follows, too, that the "validity" of the laws made by the people's elected representatives is to be tested by constitutional litigation in the courts and not by defiance of mayors, governors, and policemen. This means as to most matters—all matters, that is, outside the relatively limited scope of federal constitutional law [19]—that existing laws are to be obeyed, however reluctantly, until the rules are changed by legislative action.

The choice of values implicit in constitutional government is based on a belief that the inconvenience or irritation of conforming our behavior to laws we may consider unsound, outmoded, or unfair is far less an evil than the disruption attendant upon widespread resistance to law. A reformer working within the limits of constitutionalism will hope for change, and use his every political resource to make that hope come true, but, in the meantime, he adheres to the view of better bad law than no law at all. So we would have said, fifteen or twenty years ago, that civil disobedience had become an exercise for nuts—like Miss Vivian Kellems resisting social security taxes, or Joe Gould exercising his God-given right to cross the streets always against the stop light, or the Doukhobors stripteasing across the border in Canada—and was wholly outmoded as a major technique of social action in the United States.

This view has changed abruptly since 1961, the summer of the Freedom Riders. The Supreme Court's decision in *Brown v. Board of Education* [20] had been on the books for nine years, yet painfully little progress had been made towards educational and political equality, particularly in the states of the South. "Ninety-nine parts deliberation to one part speed!" This was the gibe, and it was basically true. So a younger civil rights leadership turned from the courts to the streets, from constitutional adjudication to massive nonviolent protest and resistance as the grand strategy for redress of the historic injustice. It was an improbable army, sometimes divided in its leadership and strangely assorted in its rank and file. As would be expected, its rhetoric was improvised and eclectic: a mixture of Gandhi's nonviolence, Thoreau's duty to stand against injustice, and St. Thomas' carefully measured denial of the obligation of unjust law.

But there was nothing cloudy about the results. More was done for racial justice in the seven years after 1961 than in the ninety-six years that followed the Civil War. Not even the filibuster could contain the force exerted. The triumph of social activism is recorded in the Civil Rights Act of 1964 and the Voting Rights Act of 1965, and our political society will never be the same again. If civil disobedience accomplished all this, or is thought of as wholly or largely responsible for it, no wonder that those who think they have simple solutions for complex social problems see it as the ultimate and irresistible weapon, a kind of political equivalent of the hydrogen bomb.

The tactic of resistance so remarkably effective for the civil rights movement was soon extended to new areas of social protest. Some of the carry-over doubtless was due to the circumstance that many of the leaders of the new, largely student, protest groups were alumni of the civil rights movement with on-the-job training in nonviolence and other resistance techniques. But there was more to it than mere continuity of personnel; civil disobedience was so closely identified with the civil rights movement that it conferred a certain dignity by association upon those who engaged in it. Even now, if we encounter a group of young men and women sprawled out on a pavement or blocking a building entrance, we are likely to draw the immediate inference that they must be there for some noble purpose. Resistance movements, from Berkeley to Columbia and at points in between, have all, consciously or unconsciously, exploited the great good will earned by the civil rights movement.

Civil disobedience is front page news, and press accounts may have given an exaggerated idea of its present incidence and extent. What we have is perhaps a brush fire, but brush fires can get out of control. What can be said, here at the brief end of a series of lectures on the efficacy of law, by way of analysis and commentary on the phenomenon?

Let it be noted, at the outset, that the civil rights movement, seriously examined, does not establish either the theoretical legitimacy or the political effectiveness of civil disobedience as an across-the-board tactic of social action. It was, as we lawyers say, a clearly distinguishable case. The grievance was monstrous and unique in

American history. The obligation to obey law rests, in a democracy, squarely on the assumption that the obliged citizen will have had the right to participate, even if unsuccessfully, in the lawmaking process. Yet the Negro, at least in the South, was an "outsider," systematically excluded from participation in the legal order against which he finally offered his resistance. I suggest, too—and this is the most important point of all—that the civil rights movement was far less a challenge to law than an appeal to law, an assertion of the law of the national Constitution, as interpreted by the Supreme Court, against the conflicting orders, statutes, and ordinances of dissident state governors, legislators, mayors, and sheriffs. Governor Faubus, Governor Wallace, and Governor Barnett were, in great matters at least, far more civilly disobedient—might I say uncivilly disobedient? —than Martin Luther King.[21] The local prohibitions against which civil rights disobedience was directed were, by and large, either plainly unconstitutional under the Fourteenth Amendment or at least arguably so. This ingredient—less infidelity to law than assertion of law— gave the civil rights movement its unique legitimacy and, more to the point, its practical efficacy.

The explanation just offered concerning the legitimacy and effectiveness of the civil rights movement cannot, with any semblance of reason, be appropriated by those who insist that civil disobedience is an appropriate political tactic against the requirements of any law with which they happen to disagree. The increasingly familiar claim that disobedience of law is itself a "civil liberty" is pure double-talk; civil liberties exist only within the context of constitutionalism, and obedience to law, until law is declared unconstitutional in court adjudication or changed by proper legislative action, is an essential article of constitutional faith. The civil disobedient, except in the most unusual of circumstances, must rest his case on the philosophical proposition that he has higher duties in conscience than he owes to the state, and he confuses and cheapens the morality of his position by offering legalistic arguments to the effect that a legal precept is somehow "invalid" *qua* law when it goes against the grain of his social and political conviction.

It is not my nature to view things with alarm, but what worries me most about the rhetoric of contemporary civil disobedience is that it refuses to draw distinctions as to relative evil and so asserts that disruptive means that are morally and philosophically justifiable against Adolph Hitler or Jim Crow are proper, too, against inconvenient rules and regulations to which one happens to object. To do this is to forget Reinhold Niebuhr's admonition that questions of relative good and evil are the essential stuff of the political order.[22] Society, if its citizens are wise and tolerant, will deal dispassionately, even gently, with the use of civil disobedience as a political tactic in situations its practitioners deem profoundly unjust, but society cannot tolerate use of the technique as one for all seasons and all occasions. Such a concession would be the end of legal obligation in contemporary society. And the death of legal obligation can be the end of the supremacy of law.

What, then, does prudence require of the prosecuting officials and judges who are charged with enforcement of laws that some passionate minority refuses to obey? [23] Law's officers have a wide range of discretion in the imposition of sanctions: imprisonment, fine, suspended sentence, simple reprimand. How are they to make the punishment fit the wholly untypical crime, and criminals, of civil disobedience? We are back now where we began. The rule of law is the product of the combined workings of legal obligation and legal coercion. These are the levers the law employs, and how is the decision-maker to proceed when obligation fails and sanctions cease to deter?

Civil disobedience, you see, is not just another form of political action, any more than Alexander's use of his sword to cut the rope of Gordius was just another way of untying knots. Civil disobedience asserts a claim much like John C. Calhoun's theory of interposition, the idea of the concurrent majority. But the advocate of civil disobedience, however high-minded he may be, is far more anti-democratic than Calhoun, because he interposes not his state's claim but his own between the majority will and its achievement. There is no majority, he contends, unless he and his fellows concur.

Thus, as has occurred so often in history, the political virtue of critical intelligence moves almost imperceptibly to the deadly sin of pride. That is the nature of tragedy —nobility of motivation destroyed, as Creon and Savonarola and Saint-Just [24] were, by stiffnecked perfectionism and self-righteousness. All social life is an accommodation. We do not live alone. Legal obligation is not simply a gesture of courtesy to the state; it is the consideration we exchange with other citizens as the price of living together.

I hope, more than I have ever hoped anything, that the tragedy will not come, that the confrontation of violence against law, anarchy against constitutionalism, will not undermine the structure of ordered liberty that men of law have built and maintained for the many centuries. Majorities—white majorities, over-thirty majorities, power-holding majorities, however you want to cut it —must be generous, dispassionate, and more understanding of the pent-up frustrations of black people, of poor people, of young people, of people who hate the Vietnam war. In the interest of social reconciliation, every concession should be made, save one.

Politically organized society will not because it cannot concede that its laws carry no obligation. This, believe me, is both an old man's doctrine and a young man's hope for a free and improving future. Society will not because it cannot concede that private individuals and private groups can choose the laws they will obey as they choose the shirts they buy, liking this one and rejecting the next. For then, as the contagion spreads, there is no law. And where there is no law, there is no liberty. And where there is no liberty, the people perish.

NOTES

I. MAKING LAWS AND INFLUENCING PEOPLE: THE PROVINCE OF JURISPRUDENCE AND THE WORLD OUTSIDE

1. Austin, THE PROVINCE OF JURISPRUDENCE DETERMINED 134 (Hart ed. 1954).
2. Kelsen, GENERAL THEORY OF LAW AND STATE 113 (1945).
3. "Law may most illuminatingly be characterized as a union of primary rules of obligation with such secondary rules [of recognition, of change, and of adjudication]." Hart, THE CONCEPT OF LAW 91 (1963).
4. Gray, THE NATURE AND SOURCES OF THE LAW 152 (Beacon Press ed. 1963).

5. Ehrlich, *The Sociology of Law* (trans. Isaacs), 36 Harv. L. Rev. 130, 131 (1922).
6. 42 U.S.C. sec. 2000a
7. Pound, *A Survey of Social Interests*, 57 Harv. L. Rev. 1 (1943).
8. Hand's version of social interest theory is more hard-boiled, and so probably more realistic, than Pound's. Witness Hand's definition of democracy as "a political contrivance by which the group conflicts inevitable in all society should find a relatively harmless outlet in the give and take of legislative compromise." THE SPIRIT OF LIBERTY 204 (1954). His characterization of law is in the same vein: "For the law is no more than the final expression of that tolerable compromise that we call justice, without which the rule of the tooth and claw must prevail." *Id.* at 87.
9. "The prophesies of what the courts will do in fact, and nothing more pretentious, are what I mean by the law." Holmes, *The Path of the Law*, 10 Harv. L. Rev. 457, 461 (1897).
10. Frank, *Cardozo and the Upper-Court Myth*, 13 Law and Contemp. Prob. 369, 384 (1948).
11. Pound, *Law in Books and Law in Action*, 44 Am. L. Rev. 12 (1910).
12. Llewellyn, *A Realistic Jurisprudence—The Next Step*, 30 Colum. L. Rev. 431, 449–53 (1930).
13. Ehrlich, *supra* note 5.
14. Kelsen, *supra* note 2, at 42.
15. Austin, *supra* note 1, at 1 and 2.
16. "At the very heart [of the 'behavior approach'], I suspect, is the behavior of judges, peculiarly that part of

their behavior which marks them as judges—those practices which establish the continuity of their office with
their predecessors and successors, and which mark their
official contacts with other persons . . ." Llewellyn,
A Realistic Jurisprudence—The Next Step, 30 Colum.
L. Rev. 431, 464 (1930).
17. Frank, *supra* note 10. And see his COURTS ON TRIAL
222–24 (Atheneum ed. 1963). Judge Frank's "fact skepticism" and his "upper-court myth" are discussed in
Jones, *The Trial Judge—Role Analysis and Profile* in
THE COURTS, THE PUBLIC, AND THE LAW EXPLOSION 125,
130 (Jones ed. 1965).
18. I–II SUMMA THEOLOGICA, Q. 96, art. 4, in THOMAS
AQUINAS: TREATISE ON LAW 97 (Gateway ed. No.
6007).
19. Cahn, THE SENSE OF INJUSTICE—AN ANTHROPOCENTRIC
VIEW OF LAW (1949).
20. "In order that a law obtain the binding force which is
proper to a law, it must needs be applied to the men
who have to be ruled by it. Such application is made by
its being notified to them by promulgation. Wherefore
promulgation is necessary for the law to obtain its
force." Thomas Aquinas, I–II SUMMA THEOLOGICA, Q.
90, art. 4, *supra* note 18, at 10.
21. "In a system thus constructed upon this plan, a man need
but open the book in order to inform himself what the
aspect borne by the law bears to every imaginable act
that can come within the possible sphere of human
agency: what acts it is his duty to perform for the sake
of himself, his neighbour or the public: what acts he has
a right to do, what other acts he has a right to have oth-

ers perform for his advantage: whatever he has either to fear or to hope from the law." Bentham, THE LIMITS OF JURISPRUDENCE DEFINED 343 (Everett ed. 1945).

22. Pers. Prop. Law sec. 402 (1957).

23. On the more recent state of affairs as concerns private supportive action in the antitrust field, see Loevinger, *Private Action—The Strongest Pillar of Antitrust*, 3 Antitrust Bull. 157 (1958). The cases, chiefly from the 1960's, are collected under the heading "Enforcement by Private Parties" in Handler, CASES AND MATERIALS ON TRADE REGULATION 1236–1304 (4th ed. 1967).

24. See Note, *Parties Plaintiff in Civil Rights Litigation*, 68 Colum. L. Rev. 893 (1968).

25. Llewellyn, *supra* note 12, at 452.

26. Sirkin v. Fourteenth Street Store, 124 App. Div. 384, 108 N.Y.S. 830 (1908).

27. Watts v. Malatesta, 262 N.Y. 80, 186 N.E. 210 (1933).

28. Bergin and Haskell, PREFACE TO ESTATES IN LAND AND FUTURE INTERESTS 18 (1966).

29. Hellerstein, TAXES, LOOPHOLES AND MORALS (1963).

30. See, e.g., Patterson, *An Apology for Consideration*, 58 Colum. L. Rev. 929, 936–38 (1958).

31. E.g., in *The Path of the Law, supra* note 9, at 457 and 459.

32. I–II SUMMA THEOLOGICA, Q. 95, art. 1, *supra* note 18, at 75.

33. Kelsen, *supra* note 2, at 19.

34. Holmes, *supra* note 9, at 470.

35. Bentham, THE THEORY OF LEGISLATION 31–32 and 326 (Ogden ed. 1931). I am borrowing here from the perceptive analysis, "Bentham's Theory of Sanctions," in

Patterson, JURISPRUDENCE: MEN AND IDEAS OF THE LAW 450 (1953).

36. "Every part of the [criminal justice] system is undernourished. There is too little manpower, and what there is is not well enough trained or well enough paid. . . . To lament the increase in crime and at the same time to starve the agencies of law enforcement and justice is to whistle in the wind." *The Challenge of Crime in a Free Society,* Report of the President's Commission on Law Enforcement and Administration of Justice (1967). And see THE COURTS, THE PUBLIC, AND THE LAW EXPLOSION, *supra* note 17, at 2–3 and 85–123.

37. On the lively controversy set off by Devlin, THE ENFORCEMENT OF MORALS (1959), see, e.g., Hart, LAW, LIBERTY AND MORALITY (1963); and Nagel, *The Enforcement of Morals,* Humanist, May/June 1968, 20–27.

38. "If we are going to be able to afford a system of administration of criminal justice which even approximates our declared ideals, we must keep to the minimum the areas of human conduct that are regulated by the imposition of criminal sanctions. Barrett, *Criminal Justice—The Problem of Mass Production* in THE COURTS, THE PUBLIC AND THE LAW EXPLOSION, *supra* note 17, at 122.

II. PRECEPTS AND CONSEQUENCES: THE UNEVEN CORRESPONDENCE OF LAWMAKING PURPOSE AND SOCIAL OUTCOME

1. Nagel, THE STRUCTURE OF SCIENCE: PROBLEMS IN THE LOGIC OF SCIENTIFIC EXPLANATION 472 (1961).
2. *"Some* diagnosis of *some* type-situation remains the essence of case law appellate judging." Llewellyn, THE COMMON LAW TRADITION: DECIDING APPEALS 429 (1960).
3. Stone, *Some Aspects of the Problem of Law Simplification,* 23 Colum. L. Rev. 319, 325 (1923).
4. Jones, *Statutory Doubts and Legislative Intention,* 40 Colum. L. Rev. 957, 971–2 (1940).
5. Zeisel and Callahan, *Split Trials and Time Saving: A Statistical Analysis,* 76 Harv. L. Rev. 1606 (1963).
6. Rosenberg, *Court Congestion: Status, Causes, and Proposed Remedies,* in THE COURTS, THE PUBLIC, AND THE LAW EXPLOSION 30, 48 (Jones ed. 1965).
7. Rosenberg, THE PRETRIAL CONFERENCE AND EFFECTIVE JUSTICE (1964).
8. *Id.* at 69.
9. *Id.* at 70.
10. Kalven and Zeisel, THE AMERICAN JURY (1966).
11. Arnold, THE FOLKLORE OF CAPITALISM (1937). But *cf.* Arnold, THE BOTTLENECKS OF BUSINESS (1940).

12. Wolfman, *Federal Tax Policy and the Support of Science*, in LAW AND THE SOCIAL ROLE OF SCIENCE 25, 35–36 (Jones ed. 1967).
13. R. v. Dudley and Stephens, 14 Q.B.D. 273 (1884).
14. Ehrlich, *The Sociology of Law* (trans. Isaacs), 36 Harv. L. Rev. 130, 138–39 (1922). For a sensitive criticism of Ehrlich's conception of "living law," see Patterson, JURISPRUDENCE: MEN AND IDEAS OF THE LAW 79–81 (1953).
15. On the genetic fallacy, see Cohen and Nagel, AN INTRODUCTION TO LOGIC AND SCIENTIFIC METHOD 388–90 (1934).
16. Pound, *Law in Books and Law in Action*, 44 Am. L. Rev. 12 (1910).
17. Nagel, *supra* note 1, at 472.

III. CONSTITUTIONALISM AND DISOBEDIENCE: THE LAW AND POLITICS OF DOMESTIC TRANQUILITY

1. "For historical reasons, administration has been the weak point of our common-law polity. England had a strong central government at an earlier date than the rest of the modern world. England had also strong courts of general jurisdiction before her neighbors. Hence before there was much call for administration of a modern type, need had been felt of putting checks upon the English crown in the interest of the individual and of the local community, and strong courts were at hand to

impose them. The tendency thus acquired by our law was intensified during the seventeenth-century contests between courts and crown and was still further intensified by the conditions of the formative period of American law." Pound, *Justice According to Law*, 14 Colum. L. Rev. 1, 22 (1914).

2. Wyzanski, *Constitutionalism: Limitation and Application* in GOVERNMENT UNDER LAW 473, 482 (Sutherland ed. 1956).
3. Jones, *The Rule of Law and the Welfare State*, 58 Colum. L. Rev. 143, 144–45 (1958).
4. This third lecture is, in part, a development of ideas first sketched out in a brief paper read before the American Philosophical Society on April 23, 1966. Jones, *Civil Disobedience*, 111 Proceedings Am. Phil. Soc. 195 (1967).
5. *The Challenge of Crime in a Free Society*, Report of the President's Commission on Law Enforcement and Administration of Justice (1967).
6. (1968). The National Advisory Commission on Civil Disorders was established by President Johnson on July 29, 1967. Executive Order No. 11, 365.
7. I–II SUMMA THEOLOGICA, Q. 100, art. 9, in THOMAS AQUINAS: TREATISE ON LAW 109 (Gateway ed. No. 6007).
8. "Municipal law is properly defined to be 'a rule of civil conduct prescribed by the supreme power in a state, commanding what is right and prohibiting what is wrong.'" 1 COMMENTARIES 44 (1765).
9. In his 1966 Rosenthal Lectures, published as THE SUSPECT AND SOCIETY (1967), Justice Walter V. Schaefer

provides a wise and searching appraisal of *Escobedo v. Illinois* (378 U.S. 478, 1964) and the other United States Supreme Court decisions in point and advances a proposal designed "to supply a rational adjustment of the needs of society and those of the individual" (at 81). And see Friendly, *The Bill of Rights as a Code of Criminal Procedure*, 53 Calif. L. Rev. 929 (1965).

10. THE CHALLENGE OF CRIME IN A FREE SOCIETY, *supra* note 5.

11. I–II SUMMA THEOLOGICA, Q. 96, art. 4, *supra* note 7, at 97.

12. THE CHALLENGE OF CRIME IN A FREE SOCIETY, *supra* note 5, at 6.

13. Hand, *The Speech of Justice*, 29 Harv. L. Rev. 617, 619 (1916).

14. REPORT OF THE NATIONAL ADVISORY COMMISSION ON CIVIL DISORDERS, 10 (Bantam ed. 1968).

15. MacIver, AS A TALE THAT IS TOLD 213 (1968).

16. *Supra* note 14, at 226.

17. E.g., in *Civil Disobedience, supra* note 4, at 195–96.

18. The same distinction is suggested in Fortas, CONCERNING DISSENT AND CIVIL DISOBEDIENCE 30–31 (1968).

19. Justice Fortas, in my judgment, conveys a somewhat exaggerated impression of the role of judicial review in the preservation of constitutionalism. See *supra* note 18, at 30. Judicial review of the constitutionality of legislation is doubtless the distinctive institution of our constitutional order, but Americans, particularly American lawyers, must be careful not to equate constitutionality with adjudicability.

20. 347 U.S. 483 (1954). For a brief account of the "after-life" of *Brown v. Board of Education,* see 2 AN AMERI-CAN PRIMER 908–11 (Boorstin ed. 1966).

21. "And what were the first two instances in recent times when it was necessary to call out Federal troops to enforce the law? I need not remind you that these were in Arkansas and Mississippi; and a similar episode was narrowly averted in Alabama only because of the calm determination of the then Deputy Attorney General Nicholas Katzenbach. In each case, it was the chief executive officer of the State who was defying the law, supported by large masses of citizens. When the law is so honored in the breach, often with the full support of local public officials, should we be surprised that pleas for law observance fall on deaf ears?" Griswold, *Masses of People,* address at annual meeting of The American Law Institute, May 24, 1968.

22. Niebuhr, AN INTERPRETATION OF CHRISTIAN ETHICS 131 (Living Age ed. 1956).

23. See Dworkin, *On Not Prosecuting Civil Disobedience,* New York Review, June 6, 1968, pp. 14–21, in which the author arrives at the "general conclusion that we have a responsibility towards those who disobey the draft laws out of conscience, and that we may be required not to prosecute them, but rather to change our laws or adjust our sentencing procedures to accommodate them" (at 21). I disagree with Professor Dworkin at several points in his discussion but greatly admire the incisiveness and intellectual integrity of his analysis.

24. "In the stifling heat of Paris in July, Saint-Just, ostensibly rejecting reality and the world, confesses that he

stakes his life on the decision of principles . . . But virtue, in that it has too much pride, is not wisdom. The
guillotine is going to fall again on that head as cold and
beautiful as morality itself. His principles do not allow
him to accept things as they are; and, things not being
what they should be, his principles are therefore fixed,
silent and alone." Camus, THE REBEL 129 (Vintage ed.
1956).

PUBLISHED ROSENTHAL
LECTURES 1948–1969

1948 Hazard, John N. "The Soviet Union and International Law," *Illinois Law Review*, XLIII, 591.

1949 Freund, Paul A. *On Understanding the Supreme Court*. Boston: Little, Brown & Co.

1951 Dawson, John P. *Unjust Enrichment, A Comparative Analysis*. Boston: Little, Brown & Co.

1952 Feller, Abraham H. *United Nations and World Community*. Boston: Little, Brown & Co.

1952 Horsky, Charles A. *The Washington Lawyer*. Boston: Little, Brown & Co.

1953 Vanderbilt, Arthur T. "The Essentials of A Sound Judical System," *Northwestern University Law Review*, XLVIII.

1954 Berle, Adolf A., Jr. *The Twentieth Century Capitalist Revolution*. New York: Harcourt, Brace.

1956 Hurst, James W. *Law and the Conditions of Freedom in the Nineteenth Century United States*. Madison: University of Wisconsin Press.

1956   Sohn, Louis B. "United Nations Charter Revision and the Rule of Law: A Program for Peace," *Northwestern University Law Review*, L, 709.

1956   Gross, Ernest A. "Major Problems in Disarmament," *Northwestern University Law Review*, LI, 299.

1956   Parker, John J. "Dual Sovereignty and the Federal Courts," *Northwestern University Law Review*, LI, 407.

1957   Ukai, Nobushige. "The Individual and the Rule of Law Under the New Japanese Constitution," *Northwestern University Law Review*, LI, 733.

1957   Papale, Antonia Edward. "Judicial Enforcement of Desegregation: Its Problems and Limitations," *Northwestern University Law Review*, LII, 301.

1957   Hart, Herbert L. A. "Murder and the Principles of Punishment: England and the United States," *Northwestern University Law Review*, LII, 433.

1958   Green, Leon. *Traffic Victims: Tort Law and Insurance.* Evanston, Ill.: Northwestern University Press.

1960   Radcliffe, Cyril John. *The Law and Its Compass.* Evanston, Ill.: Northwestern University Press.

1961   Eisenstein, Louis. *The Ideologies of Taxation.* New York: Ronald Press.

1961   Havighurst, Harold C. *The Nature of Private Contract.* Evanston, Ill.: Northwestern University Press.

1962 Pike, James Albert. *Beyond the Law:* the religious and ethical meaning of the lawyer's vocation. New York: Doubleday and Co.

1964 Katz, Wilber G. *Religion and American Constitutions.* Evanston, Ill.: Northwestern University Press.

1965 Cowen, Zelman. *The British Commonwealth of Nations in a Changing World:* law, politics, and prospects. Evanston, Ill.: Northwestern University Press.

1967 Schaefer, Walter V. *The Suspect and Society:* criminal procedure and converging constitutional doctrines. Evanston, Ill.: Northwestern University Press.

1967 Freedman, Max, Beaney, William M., and Rostow, Eugene V. *Perspectives on the Court.* Evanston, Ill.: Northwestern University Press.

1968 Donner, André M. *The Role of the Lawyer in the European Communities.* Evanston, Ill.: Northwestern University Press.

1969 McGowan, Carl. *The Organization of Judicial Power in the United States.* Evanston, Ill.: Northwestern University Press.

1969 Jones, Harry W. *The Efficacy of Law.* Evanston, Ill.: Northwestern University Press.

A NOTE ON MANUFACTURE

THE TEXT OF THIS BOOK was set on the Linotype in a face called JANSON, an "Old Face" of the Dutch school cut in Amsterdam by the Hungarian, Nickolas Kis, *circa* 1690. *Janson*'s authorship was long attributed erroneously to Anton Janson, a Hollander who had been employed in Leipzig where the matrices were rediscovered. These same mats are today in the possession of the Stempel foundry, Frankfurt, and the machine-cast version you are reading was modelled directly on type produced from the original strikes.

The book was composed, printed, and bound by KINGSPORT PRESS, INC., Kingsport, Tennessee. WARREN PAPER COMPANY manufactured the paper. The typography and binding designs are by *Guy Fleming*.

DATE DUE

OCT 3 '90	